Mag. Claudia Lichtenwagner

SMILE 3
Grammar

Englisch Übungsbuch für die
3. Klasse Mittelschule / AHS

Von Claudia Lichtenwagner bisher im G&G Verlag erschienen:

Smile Listening Comprehensions 1 (978-3-7074-1978-8)
Smile Listening Comprehensions 2 (978-3-7074-2061-6)
Smile Listening Comprehensions 3 (978-3-7074-2184-2)
Smile Listening Comprehensions 4 (978-3-7074-2187-3)

Smile 1 Grammar (978-3-7074-1306-9)
Smile 2 Grammar (978-3-7074-1307-6)
Smile 3 Grammar (978-3-7074-1308-3)
Smile 4 Grammar (978-3-7074-1309-0)

Smile Reading Comprehensions 1 (978-3-7074-1354-0)
Smile Reading Comprehensions 2 (978-3-7074-1508-7)
Smile Reading Comprehensions 3 (978-3-7074-1624-4)
Smile Reading Comprehensions 4 (978-3-7074-1846-0)

Smile Matura-Trainer Speaking Competences (978-3-7074-2080-7)

Sourire 1 (978-3-7074-1310-6)
Sourire 2 (978-3-7074-1311-3)
Sourire 3 (978-3-7074-1312-0)
Sourire 4 (978-3-7074-1313-7)
Sourire 5 (978-3-7074-1314-4)

Dieses Werk ist für den Schul- und Unterrichtsgebrauch bestimmt.

Es darf gemäß § 42 (3) des Urheberrechtsgesetzes auch für den eigenen Unterrichtsgebrauch nicht vervielfältigt werden.

SMILE – die erfolgreichste Englisch-Lernhilfenreihe
jetzt auch online auf
- Über 6.500 interaktive Übungen zu allen Grammatik-Themen
- Wiederholung, Testvorbereitung und Hausaufgaben mit automatisierten Auswertungen zur Selbstüberprüfung
- https://eduactive.at/smile

Smile

www.ggverlag.at

ISBN 978-3-7074-1308-3

36. Auflage 2025

Druck und Bindung: Imprint, Ljubljana

© 2010 G&G Verlagsgesellschaft mbH, Frankgasse 4, 1090 Wien
produktsicherheit@ggverlag.at
Alle Rechte vorbehalten. Jede Art der Vervielfältigung, auch die des auszugsweisen Nachdrucks, der fotomechanischen Wiedergabe, der Einspeicherung und Verarbeitung in elektronische Systeme sowie Text- und Data-Mining sind ohne ausdrückliche Zustimmung des Verlages gesetzlich verboten.
Gedruckt auf Papier aus geprüfter nachhaltiger Forstwirtschaft.

VORWORT

Liebe Schülerin, lieber Schüler!

Du bist mit der SMILE-Reihe schon bestens vertraut.

In SMILE 3 Grammar findest du wichtige Grammatikkapitel aus dem 3. Lernjahr übersichtlich zusammengestellt, gefolgt von zahlreichen Übungsbeispielen.

Wie gewohnt befinden sich Vokabelerklärungen und der "Key" am Ende des Buches. Gelegentlich verweise ich auf SMILE 1 Grammar und SMILE 2 Grammar, damit keine Regeln in Vergessenheit geraten.

Weiterhin viel Spaß und Freude mit Englisch!

Prof. Mag. Claudia Lichtenwagner

CONTENTS

	page
Revision: Tenses	1
It takes me ... to, took me ... to, will take me ... to	6
Conditional I	7
Conditional II	9
If or *when*	14
Other ways of talking about the future	15
Revision: *Some, any*	19
Revision: Modal verbs	20
Present perfect tense simple and progressive	25
The adverb	34
Adjective or adverb	40
Comparison of adverbs	45
Comparison of adverbs and adjectives	47
Comparison: *the ... the*	52
How to translate „werden"	54
Past perfect tense simple	60
Past perfect tense and modal verbs	64
Conditional III	65
Reported speech	69
Relative pronouns: *who, which, that, what*	78
Reflexive pronouns: *myself, yourself, himself, ...*	86
Passive	89
Words	94
Key	97

REVISION ... TENSES AND THEIR SIGNAL WORDS

Present tense simple ☺ I p 50

often
always
never
as a rule
again and again
usually
generally
normally
every day, month, week, year, morning, summer ...
sometimes
on Mondays ...
rarely = seldom
whenever

> **ACHTUNG!**
> Wenn man diese Signalwörter mit der **progressive form** verwendet, drückt man **Ärger** aus!
> She **is always criticising** me!   *Immer kritisiert sie mich!*

Present tense progressive ☺ I p 51/52

now
at the moment
at present
still
just
Look!
Listen!
Sh! The baby is sleeping!
Don't you hear? Someone is calling!

past tense simple ☺ I p 76/77

yesterday
last week (month, year)
in (1982)
in (September, winter ...)   *wenn Handlung vorbei*
on (Monday ...)   *wenn Handlung vorbei*
at (five o'clock)   *wenn Handlung vorbei*
ago
before
aufeinanderfolgende Handlungen in der Vergangenheit
wiederholte Handlungen in der Vergangenheit

past tense progressive ☺ II p 79

when / while rule
bestimmter vergangener Zeitpunkt: At three o'clock
Yesterday afternoon I was studying for my test.
between four and five ...
from eight to nine yesterday

present perfect tense ☺ II p 68

Eine Handlung hat in der Vergangenheit begonnen
und ist in der Gegenwart beendet.
Es gibt ein Resultat, eine Auswirkung.

just	lately
ever	up to now
never	recently
already	this week ...
yet, not yet	
for (Zeitstrecke)	a week, a month, a year, a long time, ages
since (Zeitpunkt)	three o'clock, Monday, the summer of 2010, May, last year, Christmas, Easter, 2008, my youth, since he was a boy ...

Going to-future ☺ II p 47

für **sichere**, nahe Zukunft, persönliche Pläne,
persönliche Absichten
sichere Wetterprognosen
I know
I'm sure
I'm certain

Will-future ☺ II p 45/46

unsichere Erwartungen, Hoffnungen, Ängste,
Warnungen, ganz spontane Entscheidungen,
formelle Ankündigungen, Zeitungsartikel,
Anweisungen
in if-Sätzen

expect
hope
think
doubt
I'm afraid
wonder
bet
warn
it is possible that
fear
worry, I'm worried
probably
possibly
perhaps
maybe
promise
In that case

DO YOU REMEMBER? – TENSES

1. I usually .... (do) my homework in the afternoon.
2. She .... (go) to Rome last year and .... (buy) a leather bag.
3. I .... (already finish) my homework, Mum.
4. While father .... (work) in the garage, mother .... (cook) in the kitchen.
5. Bob .... (sleep) too long as a rule.
6. He .... (just write) a note to his dad.
7. Mike .... (never have) his leg in plaster before.
8. The baby .... (sleep) when all of a sudden Tommy ran into the room.
9. There .... (be) yellow clouds in the sky. It .... (hail) in a few minutes.
10. Next week he .... (come) and pay us a visit.
11. I .... (not phone) him since last May.
12. In the summer of 2018 my parents .... (be) in Venice.
13. I .... (not see) my girlfriend for a long time.
14. During our holidays next summer we .... (go) to Paris.
15. Generally he .... (do) his homework carefully.
16. Look, a big fly .... (climb) up the window.
17. I .... (already do) the ironing.
18. The pupils .... (get) a good mark last week.
19. I am quite sure he .... (shout) at us in a few seconds.
20. He .... (leave) home at seven o'clock every day.
21. He .... (read) a book when his mother .... (enter) and .... (ask) if he .... (want) something to drink.
22. Whenever you .... (come) to Austria, be my guest!
23. I .... (not see) him for a long time.
24. This week Peter .... (study) a lot for his English test.
25. At this moment I .... (write) sentence number 25.
26. She .... (learn) a poem when her friend .... (come) to see her.
27. I .... (be) very fast, but my friends Tim and Bill .... (catch) me at the corner.
28. All the children .... (look forward to) the Christmas holidays now.

29. Last week somebody ………………………… (steal) all his money.
    He ………………………… (be) very unhappy then.
30. I hope that the weather ………………………… (be) fine tomorrow.
31. Whenever Mrs Franklin ………………………… (meet) me,
    she ………………………… (ask) how my mum and my dad ………………………… (be).
32. Where ………………………… (you / be) this morning?
    I ………………………… (try) to phone you three times.
33. How much money ………………………… (you / spend) on books every year?
34. How much money ………………………… (you / spend) during your holidays?
35. She ………………………… (begin) to cry when Fred
    ………………………… (step) on her toes.
36. How long ………………………… (you / stay) in Rome next year?
37. Our next English test ………………………… (be) on November 5th.
38. I promise, I ………………………… (never talk) back again.
39. Yesterday when the children ………………………… (dig) a deep hole
    in the sand they ………………………… (find) a big shell.
40. I hope you ………………………… (have) a nice time in Vienna.
41. The house ………………………… (be) still empty because the Fishers
    ………………………… (not yet arrive).
42. Ben ………………………… (have) his car since 2018.
43. Last Sunday while we ………………………… (eat) our lunch
    a swarm of bees suddenly ………………………… (attack) us.
44. The glass ………………………… (break) when Sally
    ………………………… (fill) it with hot tea three minutes ago.
45. I ………………………… (not understand) this sentence.
    What does it mean?
46. They ………………………… (never have) a worse storm in Florida.
47. All right, then. I ………………………… (pick you up) in half an hour.
48. ………………………… (you already hear) about Sue's accident?
    She ………………………… (break) her arm when she
    ………………………… (fall) down the stairs.
    Now she ………………………… (be) in hospital with her arm in plaster.
49. When Phil ………………………… (ride) his bike, a dog suddenly
    ………………………… (jump) onto the road and ………………………… (bite) him.
50. While Roger ………………………… (pack) his suitcase, Linda
    ………………………… (write) something in her diary.
51. What's that funny smell? – I think Lucy ………………………… (fry)
    some sausages.
52. Give me your binoculars! What ………………………… (he / do)?
    He ………………………… (get) out of his car, he ………………………… (take)
    a bunch of red roses and ………………………… (hurry) to her door.

IT TAKES ME ... TO   IT TOOK ME ... TO
IT WILL TAKE ME ... TO   *brauchen*

Study the following sentence patterns:

It usually **takes me** five minutes **to** get dressed.
Ich brauche für gewöhnlich fünf Minuten zum Anziehen.

It took him several weeks **to** forget her.
Er brauchte einige Wochen, um sie zu vergessen.

It takes her half an hour **to** cook lunch.
Sie braucht eine halbe Stunde, um das Mittagessen zu kochen.

How long **does it take you to** do your homework?
Wie lange brauchst du für deine Hausübung?

It took Betty three hours **to** get ready for the party.
Betty brauchte drei Stunden, um für die Party fertig zu werden.

It will take me hours and hours **to** clean up this mess!
Ich werde stundenlang brauchen, um diese Bescherung wegzuputzen!

Translate:
1. Vater brauchte zwei Stunden, um die Hemden zu bügeln.
2. Ich werde eine Stunde brauchen, um den Aufsatz zu schreiben.
3. Wir brauchten einen halben Tag, um ans Meer zu fahren.
4. Vater wird zwei Monate brauchen, um den Gartenzaun zu reparieren.
5. Gewöhnlich braucht er mehr als eine Stunde, um seinen Tee zu trinken.
6. Die Kinder brauchten einige Stunden, um die Sandburg zu bauen.
7. Wir brauchen nicht mehr als fünfzehn Minuten, um das Zelt aufzustellen.
8. Betty brauchte zwei Tage, um ihr Kleid zu nähen.
9. Die Feuerwehr brauchte drei Stunden, um das Feuer zu löschen.
10. Wir brauchten fünf Stunden, um auf den Berg zu steigen.
11. Er wird Jahre brauchen, um ihren Tod zu verschmerzen.
12. Normalerweise brauche ich zehn Minuten, um in die Schule zu gehen.
13. Oma wird zwei Stunden brauchen, um die Blumen zu pflanzen.
14. Tom brauchte eine Stunde, um den Koffer zu packen.

CONDITIONAL I

1. **Conditional I is used for general statements, facts and natural laws.**
   (*für allgemeine Aussagen, Tatsachen und Naturgesetze*)
   Bedingung ist erfüllbar.

   if + present ⇨ present

   Attention: **If can be placed at the beginning or in the middle** of the sentence.
   (*If kann am Anfang oder in der Satzmitte stehen.*)
   Steht es am **B**eginn, setzen wir einen **B**eistrich.

Examples:

If you *heat* snow, it **melts**. (*das ist immer so, allgemeingültig*)
If you *pour* oil on water, it **floats**. (*das ist immer so, allgemeingültig, Naturgesetz*)
If Tom *is* sad, he always **goes** into his room. (*das ist immer so*)
If I *have got* a problem, I **can talk** to my parents. (*das ist immer so*)
If you *close* an electric circuit, current **begins** to flow. (*Naturgesetz*)
You **can tell** me *if* you *need* me. (*das ist immer so*)
If you *leave*, please shut all the windows! (*Bitte, Aufforderung*)
If you *have got* a question, please ask me! (*Bitte, Aufforderung*)

2. **Conditional I is used for specific situations or actions.**
   (*für spezielle, bestimmte Situationen oder Handlungen*)

   if + present ⇨ future
   ⇨ can, may, must, mustn't

Examples:

If you *put on* this dress, you **will look** like your grandmother!
(*einmalige, bestimmte Situation*)
If he *is* too late, father **will be** angry. (*einmalige, bestimmte Situation*)
Will you **help** him *if* he *needs* you tomorrow? (*einmalige, bestimmte Situation*)
If you *don't stop* crying like mad, you **won't be allowed to go** / **mustn't go**
to Peter's birthday party! (☺ II p 7)
If I *don't find* my glasses, I **won't be able to read** / **cannot read**. (☺ II p 6)
If you *aren't* back before eleven, mother **will be** worried.
I **won't talk** to you any more *if* you *hurt* me again.

CONDITIONAL I – PRESENT OR FUTURE

1. If you take a taxi, you .... (catch) the train.
2. If he comes tomorrow, we .... (can) help him.
3. Mother .... (get) angry if you don't write a birthday card to Aunt Mary.
4. If you go to Italy, please .... (send) me a card.
5. If I don't wear a jacket when it rains, mum .... (always / get) really mad.
6. If you lose your cap again, you .... (not get) a new one.
7. If you like the party, ... (not go) home now!
8. If Peter really comes to my party, I .... (be) surprised.
9. Please .... (give) him the letter if he comes.
10. We .... (stay) at home if it rains like this tomorrow.
11. If you leave a bottle of wine in the freezer, it .... (burst).
12. It's the weekend, so if the children want to stay up longer, they .... (may).
13. If he quarrels with his sister, she .... (not speak) to him for a long time.
14. If you don't turn off the radio now, I .... (get) angry.
15. If you really wear these orange trousers, I .... (not go) out with you!
16. You .... (look) awful if you wear this dress tonight.
17. Father .... (be) angry if you take his car tonight.
18. My father .... (be) always angry if I take his car.
19. If you forget the cake in the oven, it .... (turn) black.
20. If you take the dog for a walk, please .... (not forget) to post my letter.
21. You .... (be) sick if you eat too much of this cake.
22. If your homework is ready, ... (hand) it in, please.
23. If the weather is fine tomorrow, we .... (make) a bike trip.
24. If you shave your head, Tony, you .... (not get) any pocket money.
25. If it snows, the roads .... (be) slippery.
26. If you forget to feed the mice again, I .... (take) them back to the pet shop.
27. She always .... (tell) her mum if there's a problem.
28. If you don't help father repair the fence, he .... (not help) you with maths in the evening.
29. If you eat too many sweets, it .... (be) bad for your teeth.

CONDITIONAL II

Conditional II is is used to express **possibility**.
(*um eine Möglichkeit auszudrücken*)

if + past tense ⇨	**would** + verb
	'd + verb
	could + verb
	might + verb

Attention: In <u>written</u> English we prefer **were** for all persons instead of **was**. (*In der Schriftsprache ziehen wir **were** der Form **was** für alle Personen vor.*)

Examples:
If I were you, I **would stop** smoking.
If he were too late, he **would have** to walk.
If I knew Peter's number, I **would call** him.
If he came tonight, **we could** ask him.
If you *studied* a bit more, you **would succeed**.
If you *tidied* your room, mum **would be** happy.
If you *used* bad language in front of your parents, they **would be** very angry.
I **would not talk** back to my father *if* I *were* you.
I**'d have** more respect for my parents *if* I *were* you.
My school marks **would be** very bad *if* I *didn't work* so hard.
If Roger *went* away, she **would cry** a lot.
I**'d be** very glad *if* you *told* me the truth.

Keep in mind: *if not* = **unless**

Examples: *If* you *don't* work harder, you will fail. =
Unless you work harder, you will fail.

If she *did not* love him, she would not help him so much. =
Unless she loved him, she would not help him so much.

CONDITIONAL II

1. If he came, I .... (be) surprised.
2. If he didn't tell me the truth, I .... (be) very sad.
3. What would you do if he .... (ask) Jane out?
4. If I .... (know) the answer, I would tell you.
5. If she forgot to post the letter, I .... (be) very angry.
6. Would you believe him if he .... (tell) you his story?
7. If she .... (know) his address, she would write to him.
8. We would do our homework if we .... (can).
9. If he were in time, we .... (can) take the first train.
10. She would cry unless he .... (help) her.
11. If she took her sleeping pills, she .... (can) sleep.
12. Unless he had an alibi, the police .... (arrest) him.
13. If a spider appeared in her sleeping room, she .... (look) frightened.
14. If Betty came downstairs, she .... (can) hear what he said about her.
15. If only we had a computer, I .... (can) use it for my homework.
16. She would be sick if she .... (drink) half a bottle of wine.
17. You would waste your time if you .... (wait) for her.
18. Unless the police found the murderer, all inhabitants of Lampshire .... (be) frightened to death.
19. If he .... (be) more careful, he would get better marks.
20. If I .... (find) your ring, I would tell you at once.
21. I would never wear this stupid hat unless my mum .... (want) me to wear it.
22. If Bill .... (not / be) so cheeky, I'd like him.
23. If you worked harder, you .... (succeed).
24. If they came now, we .... (can) go to the cinema.
25. If she .... (be) more charming, she would surely find a nice friend.
26. If he passed his exam, we .... (have) a big party.
27. Unless he loved her, he .... (not / believe) her story.
28. If he didn't love her, he .... (not / believe) her story.
29. If he missed the last bus, he .... (must / walk) all the way home.

CONDITIONAL I AND II

1. We would answer if we .... (can).
2. If he comes, we .... (can) help him.
3. If they come to us, we .... (have) much fun.
4. You .... (fall) down if you aren't careful.
5. If you don't ask her, she .... (not / help) you.
6. I will come if he .... (need) me on Friday.
7. If you want, I .... (come) in the afternoon.
8. If I were you, I .... (not / do) this.
9. He would get a good mark if he .... (work) more.
10. I will leave if you .... (not / stop) shouting.
11. I would run faster if I .... (be) you.
12. If you don't work faster, we .... (cannot) hand in the papers in time.
13. If she wrote to me, I .... (answer) her letter.
14. I would help him if he .... (ask) me.
15. If you wear that dress, you .... (look) silly.
16. If you put butter into the microwave, it .... (melt).
17. If she cut her hair, she .... (look) pretty.
18. If she cuts her hair, she .... (look) pretty.
19. I would sell the tickets if she .... (not / want) to go to the theatre with me.
20. If you pay for me, I .... (can) go on a trip with you.
21. If I get a good mark, I .... (may) go to the cinema.
22. We would speak to him if he .... (not / be) so unkind.
23. If you came to us, we .... (have) a nice time.
24. If you throw a wooden stick into the water, it .... (swim).
25. I will water your flowers if you .... (give) me the key.
26. If she .... (not / eat) so much, she wouldn't be so plump.
27. If you run like this, you .... (fall) down.
28. If Sally worked harder, she .... (can) pass the exam.
29. If Liz studied more, she .... (pass) the exam.
30. If she did her homework properly, the teacher .... (give) her a good mark.
31. I would not go now if I .... (be) Peter.
32. If you ate less, you .... (be) slimmer.
33. They .... (must) help us if they come.
34. If I had more money, I .... (can) buy a car.

35. She would be in trouble if she .... (drink) too much.
36. If he were ill, he .... (must) stay at home.
37. If the weather is fine, we .... (make) a trip.
38. If he mowed the grass, he .... (earn) some extra money.
39. Will you help him if he .... (ask) you?
40. If you open the window, the wind .... (break) it.
41. He .... (buy) me that ring if he had enough money.
42. They .... (be) silly if they didn't accept his invitation.
43. If you go through the customs, you .... (must) open your bag.
44. I'll write you a card if I .... (be) in Paris.
45. If it is so windy, I .... (stay) at home.
46. If Bob gets a present, he .... (thank) you.
47. Aunt Mary will visit us if she .... (be) healthy.
48. You'll be tired in the morning if you .... (not go) to bed now.
49. If Sam is angry with me, he never .... (talk) to me.
50. What .... (you / do) if you were in my place?
51. If you see dad, please .... (tell) him that I need the car tomorrow.
52. You won't be allowed to go to the cinema if you .... (not / do) your homework first.
53. If you tell any more lies, I .... (be) very angry indeed.
54. If Fred's story seemed true, I .... (believe) him.
55. If you stay in the sun without protection, you .... (damage) your skin.
56. I'd like to come to your party if I .... (not / be) so ill.
57. If we go to London, we .... (see) all the famous sights.
58. If Sally did not worry all the time, she .... (be) much happier.
59. If Mary buys expensive clothes again, her father .... (get) mad.
60. If he leaves now, he .... (get) to Newport in time.
61. Unless you study harder, you .... (not / pass) your driving test.
62. If the fog gets thicker, they .... (not / fly) to London.
63. What will you do if you .... (hear) the alarm?
64. If I remembered the number of the car, I .... (call) the police.
65. You .... (can) concentrate better if you didn't talk so much.

66. If Roger is late, we .... (go) without him.
67. If the farmer with the apples .... (come) again, tell him to leave forty pounds.
68. Unless Simon comes with me, I .... (probably get) lost.
69. The newspaper wouldn't print this story if it .... (not / be) true.
70. If it starts to rain, I .... (take) my umbrella.
71. If Simon did that again, I .... (must) talk to him.
72. I .... (not / swim) in that dirty water if I were you!
73. If I .... (be) Mr Clark, I would give up smoking at once.
74. What would happen if she .... (drink) too much coffee? – Her blood pressure .... (rise).
75. We will stay at home unless it .... (stop) raining.
76. If you go by train, you .... (arrive) at nine p.m.
77. If Tom left now, he .... (have) a chance to get to the station in time.
78. If he were faster, he .... (can) reach the train.
79. Sue will never learn French perfectly unless she .... (go) to France for a year.
80. If you smoke, it .... (not / be) healthy, you know.
81. If you heat ice, it .... (turn) to water.
82. If Mr Smith can't turn off the tap, his cellar .... (be) flooded.
83. If you go to Vienna, please .... (inform) me first.
84. Unless he could repair his car, he .... (must) take the train.
85. He would be able to apply for a better job if he .... (live) in a bigger town.
86. If you want to smother a flame, you .... (must) take away the oxygen.
87. She would be very sad if he .... (call) her a fool.
88. I'll come round at eight if you .... (not / mind).
89. Unless she found her key, she .... (must) call the key cutting service.
90. Her husband would forgive her if she only .... (come) home.
91. If he invited her for lunch, I think she .... (accept).
92. If you ate all that sweet stuff at once, you .... (be) sick.
93. If she .... (worry) too much, she would become nervous.
94. If you don't warm up before skiing, you .... (may) damage your knees.
95. If you shout like this, you .... (lose) your voice.

IF OR WHEN

| **When:** | für Handlungen, die **sicher** oder **immer wieder** geschehen. |

| **If:** | für Handlungen, die **vielleicht** geschehen oder für **Bedingungen**. |

Examples:

If the weather is fine tomorrow, we'll go for a walk. *(Falls es schön ist, vielleicht.)*

I'm going to meet Linda tomorrow. **When** I see her, I must tell her about Bill.
(Ich werde sie morgen treffen, das ist sicher.)

It is possible that Pat will phone me. So **if** he phones, tell him to come at nine.
(Es ist nicht sicher, dass er anruft, aber falls er anruft, sag ihm ...)

Please call me **when** you <u>are</u> back. (☺ II p 88) *(Es ist sicher, dass er/sie zurückkommt.)*

I'm thirsty. **When** I <u>come</u> home, I'll have a glass of tea. (☺ II p 88)
(Es ist sicher, dass ich heimkomme.)

I'll have some Coke **if** there's <u>any</u> left. (☺ II p 19/3)
(Es ist nicht sicher, ob noch Cola da ist.)

She always has hot milk **when** she can't sleep.
(Sie trinkt immer heiße Milch, wenn sie nicht schlafen kann.)

Fill in:

1. I'm going to spend my holidays in Greece. .... I am there, I'll buy two bottles of Metaxa.
2. There could be a letter from Bill today. .... there is, please tell me.
3. I'm going to town tomorrow. .... you need anything, phone me.
4. .... you can't help me, inform me, please.
5. .... there's snow tomorrow, we'll go skiing.
6. .... I've seen the video, you can have it.
7. He is very tired .... he gets home from work.
8. .... she moved into her new flat, we would help her.
9. What will we do .... the weather is bad tomorrow?
10. .... you go to town to meet Sally, please get me some milk.
11. .... she comes home from school she has a shower.
12. .... there are still any tickets for the concert, please get two.
13. .... we don't meet tomorrow, I'll write you a card.
14. Does anybody mind .... I smoke in the living room?
15. .... Mr Miller goes to work, he takes his umbrella with him.
16. .... you drink so much, you'll be sick tomorrow.
17. .... you aren't back at nine, mother will be nervous.

OTHER WAYS OF TALKING ABOUT THE FUTURE

1. PRESENT PROGRESSIVE

Für **persönlich geplante zukünftige Handlungen** kann anstelle der **going to-future** auch das **present progressive** verwendet werden. Um Verwechslungen mit der Gegenwart auszuschließen, sollte eine **zukunftsbezogene Zeitangabe** im Satz enthalten sein.

Examples:
What **are** you **doing** *next weekend*?
We **are staying** with Peter *tonight*.
Simon **is playing** basketball *on Thursday*.
Linda **is having** tea with Mary *tomorrow afternoon*.
I**'m meeting** Frank *at five*.
They **are getting** married *next weekend*.
We **are staying** at the sea *next holidays*.
Where **are** you **spending** your holidays *this winter*?
We **are having** a party *next Saturday*.
How long **are** you **staying** away?

Sehr häufig wird vor allem im *gesprochenen* Englisch bei **Verben der Bewegung** die **going to-future** durch das **present progressive** ersetzt. Das **present progressive** wird in diesen Fällen für **Personen** verwendet.

Examples:
Dad **is flying** to Paris *tomorrow night*.
We **are going** to the cinema *this evening*.
Liz **is coming** *tomorrow afternoon*.
Mum **is arriving** late *tonight*.
We **are leaving** *on Monday*.
Pat **is going** abroad *next year*.

2. PRESENT SIMPLE

Present simple wird verwendet, wenn man über
⇨ **Abfahrts-** bzw. **Ankunftszeiten** von Verkehrsmitteln,
⇨ **Vorstellungs-, Veranstaltungs-** oder **Konzertbeginne** spricht.
Es wird gewöhnlich **nicht** für Personen verwendet.
Vorwiegend gebrauchte Verben: *start, take off, land,*
                                  begin, leave, go back ...

Examples:
The train **leaves** at 9:15.
The plane **takes off** at 8 a.m.
The bus **goes** at 10:30.
The plane **lands** at 11 p.m.
When does the concert **begin**?

When does the tennis match **start**?
The ship **goes back** at six in the evening.
The film **starts** in a few minutes.
The train **arrives** at 8 in the morning.
(see also: ☺ II p 88)

3. FUTURE PROGRESSIVE

Future progressive wird verwendet für Handlungen, die man
zu einem <u>**bestimmten**</u> zukünftigen Zeitpunkt oder
in einem <u>**bestimmten**</u> zukünftigen Zeitraum ausführen wird.

Examples:
At this time tomorrow I'**ll be flying** to Greece.
We **will be having** lunch *from 12 to 1 tomorrow.*
On Monday next week I'**ll be lying** in the sun at the beach.
They'**ll be having** tea *at five tomorrow.*
In ten years' time he'**ll still be working** as a teacher.
When you return it **will be raining**.

4. GOING TO-FUTURE, WILL-FUTURE

For the use of the **going to-future** and **will-future** see ☺ II p 45, p 47

FUTURE

1. What .... (you do) at this time tomorrow?
2. Tomorrow Linda .... (meet) some girlfriends.
3. If he has lots of money some day, he .... (buy) a house at the sea.
4. I don't think he .... (recognise) you.
5. We .... (have) lunch with mum and dad on Friday.
6. There's a hole in my sock, mum! — All right, I .... (mend) it for you at once.
7. Our train .... (arrive) at six and .... (leave) at ten past six. So we .... (not have) enough time to buy anything.
8. At this time next year I .... (take) part in an expedition.
9. Hurry up! The last bus .... (leave) at eleven p.m.
10. Where .... (you have) lunch at midday tomorrow?
11. .... (there be) class tomorrow?
12. Mrs Smith .... (possibly send) you a parcel.
13. Father .... (travel) to England next month.
14. .... (you have) a drink now?
15. Please go and get some flowers for her as soon as the shops .... (open) in the afternoon.
16. When .... (the plane arrive)?
17. What .... (John do) with all the money from the lottery?
18. We .... (get) two mice for the children next week.
19. .... (you pass) the flower shop when you .... (take) the dog for a walk?
20. At eight o'clock tomorrow he .... (work) on the last chapter of his book.
21. Hurry up! The detective film .... (start) in two minutes.
22. Dad .... (leave) for America on Wednesday.
23. The ferry .... (arrive) at seven.
24. Wait a moment! I .... (help) you!
25. The President of Amnesty International .... (come) to Vienna in August. There .... (be) an international meeting.

26. This time next year I .... (lie) in the warm and golden sand of Greece.
27. O.K. I .... (have) a Coke and a hamburger.
28. When .... (the ship go) back?
29. If the weather .... (be) fine at the weekend, our neighbours .... (have) a barbecue party.
30. Oh yes, your blouse! I .... (iron) it at once!
31. What .... (you do) in your next holidays?
32. That .... (be) five pounds, please!
33. At 10 p.m. tomorrow Peter and dad .... (watch) the tennis match on TV.
34. He .... (leave) on the 6 o'clock plane tomorrow morning.
35. Jim drank too much. He .... (be) sick.
36. I .... (listen) to records with Linda this afternoon.
37. The conference .... (be) in ten days.
38. Do you think you .... (like) Australia?
39. That .... (be) the postman!
40. Fred .... (practise) the piano from two to three tomorrow.
41. I .... (go) shopping in some minutes.
42. Let me see! All right, I .... (take) a cup of tea.
43. When .... (the last bus go)?
44. If I go to Italy this year, I .... (buy) some spaghetti.
45. I think it .... (rain) today.
46. Don't stay up. I .... (arrive) late.
47. Please come round! We .... (have) tea at five tomorrow afternoon.
48. When you come home tomorrow, I .... (sleep).
49. Sue .... (go) to America next summer holidays.
50. Liz is pale in the face. She .... (faint).
51. I hope you .... (like) my cake.
52. When .... (the soccer match start)?
53. How long .... (dad stay) away?
54. Please let me know when the train .... (arrive).
55. Robert .... (have) his first piano lesson at this time tomorrow.
56. We must run! The last bus .... (go) at midnight.
57. The president .... (talk) on TV tonight.

REVISION ... SOME, ANY, and COMPOUNDS

For the rules see ☺ II p 18, 19

1. He hasn't got .... news from his brother so far.
2. .... sent her flowers without leaving his address.
3. Goodness me! .... fool knows the answer!
4. Which magazine would you like to read? .... will do!
5. .... has used my comb! There are still hairs in it!
6. Have you got .... that I can read on my way home?
7. He told me .... stupid lie about having an accident!
8. If there's .... in here who can speak Chinese, please inform me.
9. Don't make .... noise because mum needs .... sleep.
10. .... has lost his keys in front of the garden fence.
11. I really don't mind! Come .... day you like.
12. Are you expecting .... ?
13. Where did you find the gold chain? — .... near the park.
14. I'm sure we are going to manage .... !
15. Would you like .... sweet? — Yes, please! .... chocolate if there is ....
16. You can see hardly .... of the church. They are restoring it.
17. If she has .... problems, she can go to her mother.
18. It's too dark in here. I can't see ....
19. The money must be .... on the table! Look again!
20. She can have .... she wants from him.
21. She finished her work ....
22. She left without leaving .... message. Not even her address.
23. If .... bills arrive for me, please pay them.
24. .... more questions? Please ask .... question you like!
25. I am afraid you haven't got .... idea what he was talking about!
26. Give me .... to do. .... work will be O.K.
27. She always gets good marks ....
28. They may arrive .... day. I don't know when.
29. Is there .... new? Come on, tell us ....
30. Though it was dark I saw .... over there.
31. I heard .... at the door.
32. Which bus will take me to town? .... of them!

REVISION ... MODAL VERBS

First see ☺ II p 6, 7, 12, 89

CAN	**können, dürfen**	***Bitte, Erlaubnis** bei Familienmitgliedern* ***Anbieten**,* ***Möglichkeit**,* ***Fähigkeit ausdrücken***
Can I have the car, Dad? **Can** I put on your hat, Mum? You **can** try out my bike. **Can** I help you? It **can** be very windy in autumn. Tom **can** be very charming. **Can** she sing?		*Kann ich das Auto haben, Vati?* *Kann ich deinen Hut aufsetzen, Mutti?* *Du kannst mein Rad ausprobieren.* *Kann ich dir/Ihnen helfen?* *Es kann im Herbst sehr windig sein.* *Tom kann sehr charmant sein.* *Kann sie singen?*

COULD	**könnte**	***höfliches Angebot**,* ***höfliche Bitte**,* ***Möglichkeit, Fähigkeit***
I **could** pick you up. I **could** take you to the station. **Could** you help me? **Could** you open the window? **Could** we stop? He **could** read when he was five.		*Ich könnte dich/Sie abholen.* *Ich könnte dich zum Bahnhof bringen.* *Könntest du mir helfen?* *Könntest du das Fenster öffnen?* *Könnten wir stehen bleiben?* *Er konnte lesen, als er fünf war.*

SHALL	**sollen**	***Aufforderung**,* ***Befehl, Vorschlag***
Shall we have a drink now? **Shall** I call you at eight? **Shall** I help you? He **shall** come at once. **Shall** they stay at home?		*Sollen wir jetzt etwas trinken?* *Soll ich dich um acht anrufen?* *Soll ich dir helfen?* *Er soll sofort kommen.* *Sollen sie zu Hause bleiben?*

SHALL NOT	nicht sollen	Aufforderung, Befehl, Vorschlag
We **shall not** stay long.	Wir **sollen nicht** lange bleiben.	
He **shall not** drink too much.	Er **soll nicht** zu viel trinken.	
I **shall not** meet him again.	Ich **soll** ihn **nicht** mehr treffen.	

MAY	dürfen	Erlaubnis, sehr höfliche Bitte, Möglichkeit, Vermutung
You **may** smoke in the living room.	Sie **dürfen** im Wohnzimmer rauchen.	
May I open the window, please?	**Darf** ich bitte das Fenster öffnen?	
We **may** go to Paris next summer.	Wir fahren **vielleicht** nach Paris ...	
He **may** (**not**) be at the party.	Er ist **vielleicht** (**nicht**) auf der Party.	

Anmerkung: **may** (**not**) kann durch **might** (**not**) **ohne Bedeutungsunterschied** ersetzt werden, um **Möglichkeit** und **Vermutung** auszudrücken.

MIGHT	könnte	Vermutung, Befürchtung
You **might** make him angry.	Du **könntest** ihn zornig machen.	
You **might** be late.	Du **könntest** zu spät kommen.	
She **might** be ill.	Sie **könnte** krank sein.	
They **might** smoke too much.	Sie **könnten** zu viel rauchen.	

MIGHTN'T	könnte nicht	Vermutung, Befürchtung
He **mightn't** be there.	Er **könnte nicht** dort sein.	
We **mightn't** find them.	Wir **könnten** sie **nicht** finden.	
She **mightn't** be at home.	Sie **könnte nicht** zu Hause sein.	

MODAL VERBS and TENSES

1. I .... (eigentlich nicht sollen) eat so many sweets.
2. Mr Smith .... (nicht können) help us tomorrow. He's ill. So we .... (müssen) work all alone.
3. You .... (nicht brauchen) phone her, because she's not at home at the moment. She .... (dürfen) go to Paris with her father.
4. .... (dürfen) I help myself to another sandwich? – Of course you .... (dürfen).
5. Bob .... (müssen) work very hard for his tests last week. He .... (nicht können) go to Jim's party.
6. You .... (sollen) write her a postcard for Christmas.
7. We .... (eigentlich sollen) give up our plan. It's too silly. We .... (können) make our teacher angry.
8. You .... (sollen) do your homework at once.
9. You .... (nicht dürfen) leave your bike at the front door.
10. You .... (sollen) give back the book.
11. You .... (eigentlich sollen) give back the book.
12. You .... (können) catch a cold.
13. She doesn't want guests in her room. They .... (können) smoke too much.
14. What's that card? – It .... (können) be an invitation to Jim's party.
15. It is not sure that she is coming. She .... (können) change her mind.
16. With her new glasses she .... (eigentlich sollen) see perfectly.
17. Laura missed the train so she .... (nicht können) leave for Vienna at eight. She .... (müssen) wait for the ten o'clock train.
18. Mum, you .... (nicht brauchen) cook for me, I ate at the restaurant.
19. I know I .... (eigentlich nicht sollen) eat so much meat!
20. We .... (sollen) protect all animals.

21. He .... (nicht können) enjoy his last holiday, because he .... (müssen) stay in his hotel room because of the heat.
22. Mark .... (eigentlich sollen) be arriving by now.
23. She .... (müssen) stay in bed for two weeks now.
24. Mother .... (nicht brauchen) clean her shoes because I did it for her.
25. I .... (nicht können) meet him lately because I've been ill since last week.
26. She .... (dürfen) drink sparkling wine since she was sixteen.
27. Don't make such a noise, mother .... (können) get angry.
28. Susan .... (können) recite a very long poem when she was only three.
29. I .... (eigentlich sollen) answer her letter.
30. He .... (nicht können) find his new umbrella up to now.
31. She turned up at five, so I .... (nicht brauchen) wait for her.
32. She didn't tell him the truth, so he .... (können) be very sad.
33. Since the accident Paul .... (nicht dürfen) use his father's car again.
34. The kids .... (nicht dürfen) have a party tomorrow when their parents aren't at home because they .... (können) drink alcohol.
35. Father says we .... (nicht sollen) stay too long.
36. You .... (nicht brauchen) be scared. I'm with you.
37. We .... (nicht können) buy any trendy clothes because they were so expensive.
38. I .... (können) take you to the airport, if you want. So you .... (nicht brauchen) hurry.
39. I am worried that Pit .... (nicht können) be at the party.
40. You .... (sollen) be back at ten.
41. Mum .... (nicht müssen) do any housework tomorrow because the children will do everything for her.
42. Babs .... (nicht dürfen) read in bed last night. It was too late.
43. .... (können) you help me iron father's shirts, please?

44. You .... (nicht brauchen) worry!
    We .... (können) catch the train!
45. I .... (nicht können) believe my eyes when I saw Frank with a new racing car.
46. Linda didn't phone me. She .... (können) be ill.
47. We .... (nicht sollen) call her after ten p.m.
48. I fear he .... (nicht können) be in.
49. When .... (sollen) I pick you up?
50. Tom .... (nicht dürfen) watch TV for a week now.
51. Sally .... (nicht sollen) meet this man again.
52. You .... (nicht sollen) smoke in your room.
53. You .... (nicht dürfen) smoke in your room.
54. Bill .... (nicht dürfen) spend so much money on a new mountain bike. Father won't allow it.
55. I really .... (eigentlich sollen) leave now.
56. Tom will soon come back. You .... (nicht müssen) wait very long.
57. You .... (nicht sollen) take a taxi. It's too expensive.
58. They .... (eigentlich sollen) work more for school.
59. They .... (nicht können) go to school for a week now because they all have got a bad cold.
60. Fred .... (nicht dürfen) go away next weekend if he is too late tonight.
61. You .... (nicht brauchen) pay for it this time. I'll invite you.
62. My keys .... (können) be in the car.
63. My gloves .... (müssen) be somewhere.
64. Oh no, it .... (können) rain all day!
65. At the age of twenty-five she .... (können) be married.
66. We .... (müssen) leave early because father didn't feel well.
67. .... (sollen) I get you a drink?
68. Up to now I .... (nicht können) see a flying saucer.
69. We .... (eigentlich sollen) make our beds now.
70. She .... (nicht müssen) iron her blouses and shirts up to now. Mother has done everything for her.
71. I am sure I .... (können) do my homework on my own.
72. Tom .... (nicht dürfen) stay at home alone tomorrow.

PRESENT PERFECT TENSE
SIMPLE and PROGRESSIVE

We use the present perfect tense to express a connection between past and present or future (*um eine Verbindung zwischen Vergangenheit und Gegenwart oder Zukunft auszudrücken*).

1) PRESENT PERFECT SIMPLE FORM

For the rules and the signal words see ☺ **II p 68/69**
When we use the **SIMPLE FORM** we are **more interested** in the **result** of the action. (*Das Resultat der Handlung ist uns wichtiger als die Handlung.*) We use it for **repeated, single** and **completed** actions.
(*Wir verwenden es für wiederholte, einmalige und abgeschlossene Handlungen.*)

2) PRESENT PERFECT PROGRESSIVE FORM

The present perfect progressive is used to show that **the action itself is still going on.**
We want to **stress the duration of the action.** We are **more interested** in the **action**.
(*Die Dauerform wird verwendet, um zu betonen, dass die Handlung selbst noch andauert. Die Dauer der Handlung soll dadurch besonders hervorgehoben werden. Die Handlung selbst ist uns wichtiger als das Resultat.*)

formation: have been / has been + present participle

Examples:

I **have been working** all day.
(*Dauer soll betont werden.*)

Tom **has been lying** in bed *for* a week.
(*Er ist noch immer krank.*)

We **have been staying** in Paris *for* two weeks.
(*Wir sind noch immer dort.*)

We **have been having** a wonderful time.
(*Soll zeigen, dass z.B. der Urlaub noch weiter andauert. Könnte auf einer Ansichtskarte aus dem Urlaub stehen od. in einem Telefongespräch aus dem Urlaubsort vorkommen.*)

We **have been swimming** a lot.
(... und machen es noch immer ...)

We **have been waiting** for him *for* two hours. He hasn't turned up yet.
(Es soll die Dauer des Wartens betont werden und wir werden wohl noch weiter warten müssen, da er noch nicht aufgetaucht ist. Die Handlung dauert also in der Zukunft an.)

She **has been living** here *for* twenty-seven years. She likes it here.
(Und sie wird auch in Zukunft hier leben, da es ihr gefällt.)

I**'ve been thinking** about this problem for nearly two months now, but I can't find a solution.
(Ich werde wohl noch weitergrübeln müssen, da ich keine Lösung finde. Somit dauert die Handlung auch in der Zukunft noch an.)

I **have been writing** letters *since* seven o'clock this morning. And I still have some more to write.
(Ich werde noch weiterschreiben müssen.)

They **have been repairing** the road *for* nearly seven weeks.
(Die Dauerform bedeutet, dass die Straße noch weiter repariert werden wird.)

> **ATTENTION:**
> We do **not** use the **PRESENT PERFECT PROGRESSIVE** when we mention **how often** something has been done or the **number of things** that have been done.
> *(Wir verwenden die **Progressive** Form **nicht**, wenn wir erwähnen, **wie oft** etwas getan worden ist, bzw. die **Anzahl** der erledigten Dinge erwähnt wird.)*

Examples:
I have written **three / some** letters *this* afternoon.
(Resultat: Die drei Briefe sind fertig. / Einige Briefe sind fertig.)
He has eaten **six** sandwiches. Now he feels sick.
(Resultat: Ihm ist schlecht.)
He has dug **three** holes.
(Die drei Löcher sind als Resultat sichtbar.)
I have phoned **five times** *this* morning.
He has knocked **three times**.
He has read **30** pages of his book *this* afternoon.
Tom has won for the **third time** now! I can't beat him!
She has written her **third** book now.
Chris has shot his **second** film.
Ben has scored his **twentieth** goal *tonight*!

> **ATTENTION:**
> Some verbs are **not used** in **PROGRESSIVE** FORM even if the action is still going on. They are normally **only used** in SIMPLE FORM!
> (*Manche Verben werden **nicht** in der **Progressive** Form verwendet, auch wenn die Handlung noch andauert. Sie werden normalerweise in allen Zeiten **nur** in der **Simple** Form verwendet.*)

love	*lieben*	know	*wissen*
like	*gern haben*	understand	*verstehen*
hate	*hassen*	forget	*vergessen*
dislike	*nicht mögen*	remember	*sich erinnern*
adore	*sehr mögen*	realize	*bemerken*
wish	*wünschen*	notice	*bemerken*
want	*wollen*	recognize	*erkennen*
prefer	*vorziehen*	mean	*glauben, meinen*
desire	*ersehnen*	think	***glauben, meinen***
refuse	*ablehnen*	believe	*glauben, meinen*
be	*sein*	suppose	*vermuten*
care	*sich kümmern*	forgive	*vergeben*
need	*brauchen*	last	*dauern*
see	*sehen*	belong	*gehören*
hear	*hören*	own	*gehören*
smell	*riechen*	possess	*besitzen*
find	*finden*	have	***besitzen***
lose	*verlieren*		

Study the difference:

I have always thought him kind and generous.
think = glauben, meinen ⇨ *nur simple form möglich*

I have been thinking about my future plans for 2 months now.
think = nachdenken ⇨ *progressive form möglich*

He has had his car since 2018.
have = besitzen ⇨ *nur simple form möglich*

We have been having a wonderful time.
have = haben ⇨ *progressive form möglich*

Present Perfect Simple or PROGRESSIVE

1. Where is Pamela? — She .... (go) on holiday.
2. .... (you ever be) in Hawaii?
3. Poor Paul! He .... (just drink) a glass of rum. Now he feels terribly sick.
4. She .... (not speak) French for ten years. I fear she will have difficulties in France.
5. Ben .... (try) to learn Chinese, but it is too difficult for him.
6. Poor John! He .... (lie) in bed for two days. He is still ill.
7. He .... (stay) at the Holiday Club for two weeks. He loves it there.
8. They .... (know) each other for twelve years now.
9. What .... (you / do) all afternoon? I .... (work).
10. They .... (eat) lunch since twelve o'clock. I hope they'll soon finish eating.
11. They .... (jog) all morning. Now they are exhausted.
12. The climbers .... (try) to find their way for hours. They .... (lose) their way in the snowstorm.
13. How long .... (you go) to school? — For eight years now.
14. How long .... (you live) in Salzburg? — For five months.
15. They .... (shout) for help, but nobody .... (find) them yet.
16. .... (you write) your Christmas cards yet? — Yes, of course!
17. Liz, tidy your room! — But I .... (already tidy) it!
18. People .... (look) for the children in the wood, but they .... (cannot) find them yet.
19. We .... (live) in Vienna for six years. But now we're going to move.
20. How long .... (you look) for your cat? — Since Monday.

21. She .... (paint) the walls. Now they are white again.
22. He .... (paint) the garden fence, that's why his clothes are full of paint.
23. Tom's trousers are greasy. He .... (repair) his old bike.
24. You .... (smoke) too much recently, Charlie. You should smoke less.
25. The car is going again now. Mark .... (repair) it.
26. Somebody .... (use) all my perfume! The bottle is empty!
27. She .... (write) letters all day.
28. She .... (write) three letters to her aunts.
29. How long .... (you read) this book? – For two weeks now.
30. Jim .... (play) tennis three times this week.
31. Lucy .... (write) five postcards today.
32. How many pages of this book .... (you read)? – I .... (only read) sixty so far.
33. Mandy .... (be) crazy about Phil since kindergarten.
34. He .... (buy) three bikes so far.
35. I .... (lose) my key. Can you help me look for it?
36. You look tired. .... (you work) hard?
37. Somebody .... (break) the big plate! There's glass on the kitchen floor.
38. I .... (read) the book you gave me but I .... (not finish) it yet.
39. I .... (clean) the windows. So far I .... (clean) six.
40. There's a strange smell in here. What .... (you cook)?
41. They .... (be) married for thirteen years now.
42. Sorry, I'm late. .... (you wait) long?
43. How long .... (Charlie play the piano)? – Since he was four.
44. My father .... (always work) hard.
45. Rick .... (always see) himself as an outsider.
46. It .... (never be) easy with Linda. She .... (always be) so bossy.
47. The Millers .... (stay) in Venice for one week. The weather is great and the sea is warm.

48. Lucy .... (drive) her mum wild all day.
    She .... (cry) all the time.
49. Jim .... (take) Mandy out for six weeks now.
    He is madly in love with her.
50. She .... (keep) a diary since she was twelve years old.
51. They .... (be) in Carinthia for two weeks now.
52. They .... (stay) in Salzburg for one week now.
    It is great!
53. Bob .... (be) aggressive and jealous ever since I .... (know) him.
54. Tom! What .... (you do)? Your boots are full of mud!
55. I .... (try) to solve my problem for more than three months now.
56. I .... (just manage) to solve my problem.
    Now I know what I've got to do.
57. Mary .... (always have) fewer rights than her little sister.
58. She .... (wear) hand-me-downs since she was an au pair in London.
59. I .... (not see) Frank for ages!
60. He .... (not sleep) well for a fortnight.
    That's why he is so nervous.
61. That is the second time now that you .... (break) a cup!
62. Tom .... (dislike) spinach since he was a baby.
63. They .... (have) their wonderful house for eight years.
64. Jim .... (refuse) to go to pop concerts recently.
    He prefers classical music.
65. Hi, Sally! I .... (not see) you for ages!
    What .... (you do) all the time?
    Where .... (you be)?
66. Look! The cat .... (sit) in front of the fire since this morning.
67. Sorry, I .... (not listen)! Could you please repeat that?
68. I .... (have) a terrible headache since this morning but now it .... (stop).
69. I .... (think) about his words for four hours now. I don't know what he meant.

70. My feet hurt terribly. I .... (run) around in town the whole afternoon.
71. She .... (not be) to a restaurant for a long time.
72. They .... (own) their villa at the sea for five years now.
73. Frank .... (not find) a girlfriend yet although he .... (look for) the girl of his dreams since he was sixteen.
74. I .... (ring) the doorbell for five minutes! Where .... (you be)?
75. Mrs Leister .... (not go) out since her husband died.
76. Bill .... (not do) any homework since the beginning of the school year.
77. I .... (never understand) why he is in love with her.
78. I .... (ring) the bell four times now. She can't be in.
79. I .... (shout) in front of her house for one minute now. She can't be in.
80. Sue .... (be) in hospital with a broken leg for two weeks now.
81. I .... (not hear) anything about his sister for ages.
82. Mrs Smith .... (not hoover) her carpets for two weeks. They are quite dirty now. She .... (lie) in bed with a flu.
83. This old tree .... (stand) in this corner of the garden for as long as we .... (live) here.
84. I .... (send) her three letters but she .... (not yet answer).
85. Be quiet! The baby .... (sleep) for four hours now.
86. Our teacher .... (teach) in this school since 1999.
87. This vintage car .... (belong) to Uncle Mark since 1942.
88. He .... (not buy) a new coat for fifteen years. That's why he looks so old-fashioned.
89. I'm terribly worried. We .... (look for) the right way for two hours now, but we .... (not yet find) it.

90. It .... (rain) since Monday last week. I fear it'll stay bad over the weekend.
91. Ben .... (take) Mary out to the cinema recently.
92. This old building .... (stand) on this square for nearly two hundred years. They are going to restore it now.
93. We .... (stay) at the same camping site in Carinthia for five years now. We love it here and we're going to come again next year.
94. Mum .... (bake) biscuits for two hours. She's going to bake lots more.
95. Mum .... (bake) biscuits for two hours. Now she is ready.
96. I .... (try) to phone Peter five times this morning. He isn't at home.
97. Connie .... (look for) good-looking boys on the beach for nearly a week, but she .... (not see) any.
98. Mary .... (get) a nice suntan since she .... (be) at the sea.
99. They .... (build) a new bridge for ten weeks now and they won't finish it until next spring.
100. It .... (rain) for three weeks now. That's why I .... (cannot) do any work in the garden up to now.
101. I .... (study) all the rules. Now I know them by heart.
102. I .... (want) to buy a racing car all my life. But it's too expensive.
103. He .... (adore) her since he was a little boy. He still loves her.
104. Sh! Father .... (have) a wonderful sleep since midday. Don't wake him up.
105. Tom .... (try) to find the hole in his tyre for half an hour now. He can't find it.
106. She .... (not care) for her old friends since her marriage.
107. He .... (refuse) to smoke ever since I .... (know) him.
108. He .... (always be) a fair player since he .... (be) a member in our team.
109. Mother .... (try) to repair her car in the garage the whole afternoon. Now she is waiting for dad to help her.
110. What .... (you do) Dad? – I forgot the milk on the stove.

PRESENT PERFECT SIMPLE OR PROGRESSIVE

On the telephone:

Linda: Hi, Pam! This is Linda speaking.

Pam: Hi, Linda! Great to hear from you! How are you? Are you enjoying yourself?

Linda: Oh, yes, I .... (have) a wonderful time up to now. The weather is really great with lots of sunshine. I .... (be) at the beach every day.

Pam: .... (you snorkel)?

Linda: Yes, of course, and I .... (dive) a lot and I .... (play) beach volleyball with a friend.

Pam: Friend? Tell me, ... (you find) the boy of your dreams yet?

Linda: Don't be so nosy!

Pam: Come on, tell me your little secret! What .... (you do) all the time?

Linda: We .... (have) lots of fun together.
We .... (talk) a lot.
We .... (lie) in the sun and
we .... (get) a nice suntan.
We .... (sail) a lot and
we .... (go) to the bar at the beach.

Pam: Sounds great! And in the evenings? What .... (you do) at night?

Linda: We .... (be) together till midnight every day.
We .... (run) along the beach
or .... (walk) in the moonshine.

Pam: How romantic!

Linda: We .... (hold) hands and ...

Pam: And what? .... (he / try) to kiss you yet?

Linda: Yes, we .... (kiss) all the time.
He's really very nice and charming and I .... (be) madly in love with him since I first met him. You can't imagine, he looks wonderful! ....

THE ADVERB

When must we use an adverb?

(Wann müssen wir ein Adverb verwenden?)

a) adverb + verb

Das Adverb bestimmt, beschreibt hier ein **Verb** näher.

Examples:
He writes **carefully**.
verb   adverb

He sold his car **quickly**.
verb   adverb

b) adverb + adjective

Das Adverb beschreibt hier ein **Adjektiv** näher.

Examples:
His car was **horribly** expensive.
adverb   adjective

The price was **terribly** high.
adverb   adjective

c) adverb + adverb

Das Adverb beschreibt hier ein **Adverb** näher.

Examples:
They played **pretty** badly.
verb   adverb   adverb

He writes **awfully** carelessly.
verb   adverb   adverb

Adverbs ending in -ly:

careful	— carefully	*sorgfältig*
final	— finally	*endlich*
full	— fully	*völlig*
fantastic	— fantastically	*fantastisch*
honest	— honestly	*ehrlich*
true	— truly	*wirklich*
due	— duly	*ordnungsgemäß*
shy	— shyly	*scheu*
dry	— dryly (drily)	*trocken*
capable	— capably	*fähig*
possible	— possibly	*möglicherweise*
gentle	— gently	*sanft*
terrible	— terribly	*schrecklich*
probable	— probably	*wahrscheinlich*
nice	— nicely	*nett*
extreme	— extremely	*äußerst*
happy	— happily	*glücklich*
easy	— easily	*leicht*
whole	— wholly	*völlig*
early	— early	*früh*
daily	— daily	*täglich*
weekly	— weekly	*wöchentlich*
monthly	— monthly	*monatlich*
yearly	— yearly	*jährlich*

Way / manner / fashion:

Adjektive, die bereits ein -ly haben, müssen als Adverb mit way, manner oder fashion umschrieben werden.

friendly	— **in a friendly way / manner / fashion**	*freundlich*
silly	— **in a silly way / manner / fashion**	*dumm*
lovely	— **in a lovely way / manner / fashion**	*nett, lieb*
lonely	— **in a lonely way / manner / fashion**	*einsam*
lively	— **in a lively way / manner / fashion**	*lebhaft*

Adverbs without -ly:

good	— **well**	
long	— **long**	Stay as long as you like.
fast	— **fast**	Don't speak so fast.
low	— **low**	*niedrig, tief (Stimme)*
straight	— **straight**	Let's come straight to the point. *(direkt)*
extra	— **extra**	
doubtless	— **doubtless**	*zweifellos*

Double forms:

Manche Adjektive haben *zwei* Adverbien mit *unterschiedlicher Bedeutung*.

hard   He works **hard**. *(schwer)*
He **hardly** works. *(kaum)* (Mind *word order*!)

near   The dog came **near**. *(nahe herzu)*
It **nearly** came. *(beinahe)* (*word order*!)

late   Bob arrived **late**. *(spät)*
We haven't met him **lately**. (*Wir haben ihn in letzter Zeit nicht getroffen.*)

fair	Paul plays **fair**. *(fair, gerecht)*
	He sings **fairly** well. *(ziemlich)* *(word order!)*
direct	He went **direct** to London. *(direkt)*
	The train goes there **direct**.
	Wait for me. I'll come **directly**. *(sofort)*
high	He went **high** up the mountain. *(hoch auf den Berg hinauf)*
	He was **highly** astonished. *(höchst)* *(word order!)*
	He is **highly** paid. *(Er ist hoch / bestens bezahlt.)*
deep	He dived **deep**.
	I was **deeply** hurt. *(zutiefst)* *(word order!)*
close	Come **closer** together. *(näher zusammenkommen)*
	He resembles his father **closely**. *(sehr ähnlich sein)*
	He watched me **closely**. *(scharf beobachten)*
dear	The house cost him **dear**. *(teuer)*
	He would **dearly** love to see her. *(äußerst gerne)*
	Victory was **dearly** bought. *(teuer erkauft)*
ready	He wears **ready**-made suits. *(Konfektionsanzüge)*
	They **readily** agreed. *(Sie stimmten bereitwillig zu.)*
short	He stopped **short**. *(Er blieb plötzlich stehen.)*
	He came **shortly** after. *(kurz danach)*
false	He played me **false**. *(ein falsches Spiel treiben)*
	He was **falsely** accused. *(zu Unrecht angeklagt)*
free	We got in **free**. *(gratis, umsonst)*
	She talked **freely**. *(ungezwungen, zwanglos)*
just	**Just** listen! *(nur, gerade, erst)*
	He was **justly** punished. *(zu Recht bestraft)*
pretty	He does it **pretty** fast. *(ziemlich)*
	You're **pretty** good.
	She was **prettily** dressed. *(hübsch gekleidet)*

> **Keep in mind:**

Folgende Ausdrücke sollst du dir merken:
(Wenn das *-ly* in Klammer ist, kannst du beide Formen
als Adverb verwenden.)

to buy cheap(ly)	*billig kaufen*
to sell cheap(ly)	*billig verkaufen*
to think highly of someone	*von jemandem eine hohe Meinung haben*
to speak highly of someone	*sich sehr positiv über jemanden äußern*
Take it easy!	*Nimm's leicht!*
to speak loud(ly)	*laut sprechen*
to speak slowly	*langsam sprechen*
to pass slow(ly)	*langsam vorbeigehen*
to drive slow	*langsam fahren*
to remember right(ly)	*sich richtig erinnern*
to be accurately informed	*richtig informiert sein*
to be incorrectly informed	*falsch informiert sein*
to be wrongly accused	*fälschlicherweise angeklagt sein*
to pronounce wrong	*falsch betonen*
to spell wrong	*falsch buchstabieren*
to guess right / wrong	*richtig / falsch raten*
to answer correctly / incorrectly	*richtig / falsch antworten*
to put / set right	*in Ordnung bringen*
to turn sharp(ly) to the left	*scharf links abbiegen*
to stay long	*lang bleiben*

No adverb after:

Nach einigen Verben wird KEIN Adverb verwendet:

feel	*sich anfühlen*	The cloth feels soft. *(weich)*
smell	*riechen*	It smells good in here.
taste	*schmecken*	The coffee tastes good.
sound	*klingen*	That sounds perfect.
look	*aussehen (wie)*	She looks nice.
be	*sein*	I am happy.
seem	*scheinen*	It doesn't seem difficult. *(schwierig)*
become	*werden*	He is becoming famous. *(berühmt)*
turn	*werden*	He turned pale. *(blass)*
grow	*werden*	She grew angry. *(zornig)*
get	*werden*	It's getting dark. *(dunkel)*
remain	*bleiben*	She remains silent. *(ruhig)*

Exceptions (Ausnahmen):

Wenn *look* eine Präposition bei sich hat (in, after, for, behind …),
also nicht *aussehen* heißt, **wird das ADVERB verwendet.**

She **looked at** me angri**ly**.	ansehen
She **looks after** the children careful**ly**.	sich kümmern
He **looks for** his key nervous**ly**.	suchen

Wenn *taste* verkosten, kosten heißt,
also nicht *schmecken,* **wird das ADVERB verwendet.**

He **tastes** the soup careful**ly**.	kosten

ADJECTIVE OR ADVERB

1. Look out of the window. It is raining .... (heavy).
2. I can do this exercise .... (easy).
3. Pit is very .... (aggressive).
4. He shouts .... (furious).
5. Hurry up! You are always too .... (slow)!
6. Yesterday I went to bed .... (early).
7. The door opened .... (slow).
8. Mother came into my room .... (quiet).
9. The baby is sleeping .... (quiet).
10. Your cake tastes .... (wonderful).
11. What he told us sounded .... (interesting).
12. She always dresses .... (pretty) .... (awful).
13. This exercise is not .... (difficult).
14. Mr Smith is a .... (pretty) .... (good) driver.
15. Our teacher always speaks .... (clear) and .... (slow).
16. I .... (hard) know him.
17. The cat .... (near) bit me when we were playing.
18. Our football team played .... (good).
19. She understands French .... (perfect).
20. She is really .... (perfect) at French.
21. I don't feel .... (fine) at the moment.
22. I have got a .... (bad) cold.
23. These apples smell .... (good). I think I'll take one.
24. Oliver can run very .... (fast / quick).
25. Please be .... (quiet) and listen .... (careful).
26. Granny didn't sleep .... (good) last night.
27. She always laughs .... (friendly).
28. You look .... (tired), Frank.
29. Mother is a .... (good) cook. She cooks .... (good).
30. Mick plays the piano .... (terrible) .... (bad).
31. Put on your coat. It is .... (extreme) .... (cold).
32. Paul is a .... (fair) .... (good) tennis player.
33. Paul is a .... (fair) and .... (good) tennis player.
34. Paul plays .... (fair) .... (good).
35. It smells .... (good) in your kitchen.
36. Peter is .... (awful) hurt about what you said.
37. These carrots are really .... (cheap).

38. The pears look .... (fresh) and .... (good).
39. The birthday cake tastes .... (good), Mum.
40. Look! That was a .... (bad) fall! Today he is skating .... (bad).
41. Mother sews .... (good).
42. Robert is watching the children .... (sad).
43. The kids dance around .... (happy).
44. She is always .... (nice) and .... (friendly) and she greets everyone .... (friendly).
45. We get the newspaper .... (daily).
46. Come here .... (quick) and listen to me .... (careful).
47. Ken is a .... (good) skater. He really skates .... (good).
48. It's getting .... (cold). Let's have a glass of .... (hot) lemonade.
49. Bob thinks that wine tastes .... (awful).
50. Let's go to The Happy Chinese Restaurant. They have got a very .... (friendly) waiter and he serves the meals .... (quick).
51. The soup doesn't taste .... (good), it's a bit .... (salty).
52. Frank doesn't dance .... (good). He always steps on my toes.
53. Lisa sings .... (beautiful).
54. Hurry up! You are too .... (slow). Can't you do your work .... (quick)?
55. Simon ran very .... (fast). He is an .... (excellent) sprinter.
56. The teacher looked at her .... (angry).
57. Eric sings .... (bad).
58. Nancy looks .... (pretty) in her new dress.
59. Please do your homework .... (careful). It's not .... (difficult) and you can do it .... (easy).
60. Rick answered .... (polite).
61. Why are you looking so .... (angry) now?
62. Chris is a bully. He often behaves .... (bad) at school and he gets .... (angry) very .... (easy).

63. Please don't .... (careless) drop your chewing gum paper on the ground.
64. This drink tastes .... (awful)!
65. Ben often behaves .... (silly).
66. You don't play .... (fair)!
67. The boy .... (near) fell into the .... (deep) water.
68. He was .... (deep) shocked by the horror film.
69. What have you been doing .... (late)?
70. Molly .... (hard) studies anything. She won't get a .... (good) mark.
71. William is a .... (high) educated man.
72. Don't go .... (near) this dog! Two days ago it .... (near) bit me.
73. Pit always plays the clown and talks .... (silly).
74. You don't work .... (hard) enough.
75. These pills taste .... (horrible).
76. Father speaks English very .... (good).
77. Mother is always .... (busy) in the morning.
78. Shut the box .... (quick)! That cheese smells .... (terrible).
79. Yesterday it rained .... (heavy).
80. Jeff hurt his leg .... (bad). He ran too .... (quick).
81. Are you .... (nervous) before a test? – No, not at all because I always study .... (careful).
82. Mr Green bought his car .... (cheap).
83. He'll .... (hard) have a chance because he doesn't work .... (hard) enough.
84. I worked .... (busy) today, but now I'm .... (tired) and am going to bed .... (quick).
85. Mrs Briggs always dresses .... (beautiful).
86. He wasn't thinking .... (clear).
87. Peter pressed my hand so .... (hard) that it hurt .... (bad).
88. Mother looked .... (happy) at the .... (nice) flowers.
89. Don't speak so .... (loud). We must go in .... (quiet) and .... (slow).

90. Mary paints very .... (good). She is a .... (good) painter.
91. Mother waved to me .... (friendly).
92. Mandy is .... (terrible) .... (stupid).
93. His new racing car was .... (horrible) .... (expensive).
94. The team played .... (pretty) .... (bad) but we got in .... (free).
95. He .... (final) knew the .... (correct) answer and answered .... (shy).
96. She is .... (complete) happy.
97. He is .... (total) in love with her.
98. The children are playing .... (happy) and .... (free) in the playground.
99. Nelly sings .... (fantastic).
100. It's .... (extreme) cold today.
101. Let's go to bed .... (early) today because yesterday we went to bed .... (late).
102. Pam cares for her cat .... (lovely).
103. Joe answered in a .... (low) voice.
104. Fred .... (near) won the first prize.
105. Uncle Mark arrived .... (late).
106. He plays the recorder .... (fair) .... (good). His fingers dance up and down .... (quick).
107. The bus goes .... (direct) to Leeds.
108. Hey, don't run away! I'll come .... (direct).
109. The plane flies .... (high).
110. Mr Grant has a .... (high) paid job.
111. Tina was .... (deep) hurt when you left.
112. Sharon resembles her mother very .... (close).
113. She would .... (dear) love to meet him again.
114. She .... (ready) helped him.
115. Don't stop .... (short), go ahead .... (quick)!
116. I was .... (high) astonished about his .... (bad) mark.
117. Tom can dive very .... (deep).
118. Jimmy watched the girl .... (close).
119. He sold his car .... (dear).

120. The old man looked .... (complete) satisfied.
121. You never come .... (straight) to the point.
122. Mr Smith spoke very .... (low).
123. He .... (doubtless) was .... (deep) moved.
124. Pit resembles his grandfather .... (close).
125. How .... (deep) can you dive?
126. He bought his vintage car .... (dear).
127. They talked .... (free) about their problems.
128. Pam was so .... (pretty) dressed and looked so .... (elegant) that the young man stopped .... (short) and looked at her .... (admiring).
129. When he is drunk he always talks .... (silly).
130. When did he arrive? – .... (short) after you came.
131. When father suggested a trip to the USA, mother .... (ready) agreed.
132. Get .... (close) together or I can't get you on the photo.
133. Linda would .... (dear) love to get married.
134. How much did you pay? – Nothing, we got in .... (free).
135. He has .... (just) left her. She was .... (terrible) jealous.
136. .... (just) you wait! I'll get you!
137. The old lady was .... (pretty) impatient.
138. Mr Miller speaks .... (high) of Mr Grant.
139. You'd better take your bad mark .... (serious). Work .... (careful).
140. Please drive .... (slow). If I'm not .... (incorrect) informed, you must turn .... (sharp) to the right now.
141. Robert played Lucy .... (pretty) .... (false).
142. The detective watched the suspect .... (close).
143. Does this bus go .... (direct) to St.Paul's?
144. They stayed a .... (long) time in the church and remained .... (silent).
145. Liz tasted the drink .... (curious) and turned .... (pale).
146. One day he will become .... (famous) with his new invention.
147. It seemed .... (difficult) but you did this exercise .... (perfect).

COMPARISON OF ADVERBS

1. with *more* and *most*

Die Adverbien auf *-ly* werden mit **more** und **most** gesteigert.

quietly	more quietly	most quietly
happily	more happily	most happily
carefully	more carefully	most carefully

2. with *-er*, *-est*

Adverbien **ohne Endung** werden mit *-er*, *-est* gesteigert.

high	higher	highest
hard	harder	hardest
fast	faster	fastest
early	earlier	earliest
long	longer	longest
low	lower	lowest
late	later	latest
fair	fairer	fairest
in a friendly way	in a friendlier way	in the friendliest way

3. unregelmäßige Steigerung:

well	better	best
badly	worse	worst
much / many	more	most
little	less	least

COMPARISON OF ADVERBS

1. Dave changed his mind .... (quick) than Sue.
   She thought a bit .... (long).
2. We walked .... (fast / quick) than usual because it was terribly cold.
3. Pit came .... (early) than we expected and he stayed .... (long) than last time.
4. This winter it is snowing .... (heavy) than last year.
5. Betty greeted us .... (friendly) than her sister.
6. Tom does his homework .... (careful) than his friend Bill.
7. Simon talks French .... (good) of all.
8. Our team ran .... (fast) and jumped .... (high) than the other.
9. The driver was .... (severe) injured than we first thought.
10. Linda sang .... (beautiful) than all the other girls and won the first prize.
11. Robert played .... (fair) of all.
12. The school team trained .... (hard) than last time and won .... (easy) than in the last match.
13. He knows everything .... (good) than her. That's why she is angry with him.
14. The bird flew .... (high) than the aeroplane.
15. Sue swam .... (slow) than all her classmates.
16. If you don't try to write a bit .... (careful), I won't read your letters any more.
17. This weekend it even rained .... (heavy) than last weekend.
18. She came in .... (silent) than yesterday in order not to wake up the baby.
19. If you want to go to the theatre, you ought to be dressed .... (elegant) than you are now.
20. Mrs Miller drives even .... (careful and slow) than her husband.
21. This year she is working .... (good) than she did last year.

COMPARISON OF ADVERBS AND ADJECTIVES

Comparison of **adjectives** see ☺ II pages 33–44

1. Please copy this exercise .... (careful) than you did the last time.
2. Stop fooling around! You ought to be .... (clever) than your little brother!
3. English is my favourite subject. I like it .... (good) than Maths.
4. Nancy is .... (tired) than I am, but I worked .... (hard) than she did.
5. Be .... (careful) than in your .... (late) test.
6. You can't read his letters. His handwriting is even .... (bad) than mine.
7. Our teacher looks .... (thin). I'm sure she's lost weight.
8. I bought a new watch. I expected it to be much .... (cheap).
9. My headache is even .... (painful) than it was two hours ago.
10. When does the .... (near) train leave for Vienna? I missed the .... (late) one.
11. Mum always works .... (busy) than I do.
12. Liz is the .... (thin) girl in our class.
13. Charlie's sister always greets us .... (polite) than he does. She is .... (friendly and nice) than her brother and I like her much .... (good).
14. Mark's test is the .... (good) in the class.
15. They ran to school .... (quick) than yesterday because they didn't want to be late again.
16. Sue eats the .... (little) of us all.
17. Mr Grant speaks .... (slow) than his wife.
18. He passed his exam .... (successful) than last year.
19. Tom plays the recorder .... (good) than last year. He's practised .... (serious) than he did before.
20. Spielberg's .... (late) film is even .... (exciting) than his .... (late) one.

21. This time your cake tastes .... (good) than last time. Some day you'll be the .... (good) cook in the whole world.
22. Observe the traffic signs .... (careful) today or you'll have to pay a fine again.
23. Speak .... (loud), I can hardly hear you.
24. If the weather gets .... (bad) than it is now, the plane won't be able to take off.
25. Since he has been married he is much .... (happy) and .... (charming) than ever before.
26. She thought she knew him .... (good) than she really did.
27. If you studied .... (hard), you would get .... (good) marks.
28. Linda has been dressing .... (pretty) since she's got a boyfriend than she did before.
29. If it rains .... (heavy) than yesterday, the fire brigade will have to pump out many cellars.
30. As we needed .... (far) information, we asked at the tourist office.
31. Who can run the .... (quick)? Tim or Pit?
32. After his holidays in Italy he was able to speak .... (fluent) than before.
33. Any .... (far) questions?
34. This perfume smells .... (nice) than the other.
35. As Sally burnt her mouth yesterday, she tasted the soup .... (cautious) than yesterday.
36. You should take this dress. You look .... (beautiful) in the blue one. Blue goes .... (good) with your hair than red.
37. I can understand Mr Winter .... (good) than his wife. He speaks .... (clear and slow) than her.
38. He paints the .... (exciting) pictures I've ever seen. He is the .... (great) artist I know.
39. Bill's dog runs .... (quick) of all.
40. She looked at me .... (sad) than ever before.
41. The twins are totally different from each other. Pam sings .... (bad) than Liz, but she is far .... (good) at languages.
42. Kate thinks John is the .... (good-looking) man she's ever seen.

43. Yuk! These flowers smell .... (awful) than rotten eggs!
44. This is the .... (bad) idea you've ever had!
45. He cared .... (much) about Linda than about Lucy.
46. His bad temper is getting .... (bad) and .... (bad) every day.
47. He is the .... (terrible) bore I've ever met.
48. We wish you all the .... (good) for your exam!
49. Jurassic Park is the .... (frightening) film I've ever seen.
50. The second band played .... (horrible) than the first.
51. Nancy has been the .... (happy) girl in the world since she met Dave three weeks ago.
52. Uncle Jim laughed .... (loud) of all.
53. I hope it will freeze .... (hard) this winter than it did last winter.
54. Sharon did her Latin test .... (bad) than the rest of the class.
55. After sleeping Frank felt .... (hungry) than after a long run.
56. Do you think that alligators are .... (dangerous) than snakes?
57. He is the .... (bad) pupil I've ever had. He doesn't understand the .... (easy) exercises.
58. We are waiting for .... (far) instructions.
59. Tom talks far .... (quick and clear) than Pit and he thinks twice as .... (fast) as he does.
60. Bob works even .... (hard) than his father and earns lots .... (much) money than he does.
61. Florida is a .... (expensive) place than Paris.
62. Grandmother is .... (easy) worried about anything than mother.
63. She ate her cake .... (greedy) than the other children.
64. Of the three brothers Simon is the .... (nice).
65. You must work .... (careful) next time to get a .... (good) mark than today.
66. Her .... (late) party was still .... (boring) than I'd expected.
67. This is the .... (terrible) meal I've ever tasted.

68. Marrying him was her .... (bad) mistake.
69. Linda found a new flat .... (easy) than her girlfriend, but it was far .... (expensive) than hers.
70. He behaved .... (selfish) than his friend and took the .... (big) slice of the cake.
71. People were dressed .... (colourful) at the carnival in Venice than in Cologne.
72. The red blouse fitted Linda .... (good) than me because she is .... (tall and slim) than I am.
73. Before tests I feel much .... (nervous) than my friend. He takes everything .... (easy) than I do.
74. At present I can sleep .... (deep) than ever before and I need .... (little) sleep than before, but I feel .... (fresh).
75. He sold the house .... (cheap) than we expected.
76. Please follow .... (close) behind! Go .... (quick)!
77. This was the .... (frightening) book I have ever read.
78. His new excuse seems .... (believable) than the last he told us.
79. We were received .... (nice) than last time.
80. He got up .... (early) than ever because he wanted to be the first at the office.
81. Sally's concert was great. She sang .... (fantastic) than ever before.
82. Our headmaster is the .... (patient) person I've ever met.
83. Simon fell again and hurt himself even .... (bad) than last time.
84. The song he has written now is the .... (awful) song he's ever composed.
85. Your coffee is the .... (good) I've ever tasted.
86. Mrs Winter sold her house .... (quick) than we all expected.
87. Last winter I caught the .... (bad) cold I have ever had.
88. Fred is able to dive .... (deep) of all the children.
89. Mr Brown's photos are the .... (interesting and exciting) that have ever been shot in an expedition.

90. The police stopped him because he was driving .... (fast and dangerous) than they allowed.
91. Mr Smith missed the .... (late) train because he couldn't find his ticket.
92. I like Robert. He is .... (nice, helpful and friendly) than all the others.
93. I won't play with you again if you don't play .... (fair).
94. She talked .... (free) about her experiences than her friend.
95. At last he bought the car .... (dear) than he wanted to.
96. Stop it! Now you are pronouncing the word even .... (incorrect) than before!
97. Let's pass .... (slow) or I won't be able to see anything.
98. Velvet feels .... (soft) than silk.
99. Classical music sounds .... (pleasant) to my ear than jazz.
100. We stayed .... (long) than we at first wanted to.
101. Your new plan sounds .... (great and realistic) than your last.
102. Please drive .... (slow). I don't think we will be .... (late) than last time.
103. Eve was dressed .... (pretty) than all her girlfriends.
104. It's getting .... (warm) day after day.
105. I like Charlie .... (good) of all.
106. Our last au-pair looked after the children .... (careful) than all the others we had had before.
107. Father was .... (angry) than ever before.
108. He eats .... (little) of us all, but he is even .... (strong) than the rest of us.
109. Congratulations! You did your work .... (appropriate) than last week.
110. They enjoyed their holidays .... (intense) than ever before.
111. He answered .... (intelligent) of all the candidates.
112. Are you in a hurry? Please stay a bit .... (long).
113. Fred was sitting in his chair .... (quiet) than Tom.
114. You really could greet us .... (friendly).
115. I eat .... (little) meat now than I did before.
116. She is .... (busy) than ever before.

COMPARISON: the ... the (je ... desto)

> **ATTENTION:**
>
> Mind the **word order:** 1. **S**ubject 2. **P**redicate
> ⇨ *Die Wortstellung weicht vom Deutschen ab*!
>
> **The** *more* he has, **the** *more* he wants.
>   subject predicate   subject predicate
>
> *Je mehr er hat, desto mehr will er.*
>   subject predicate   predicate subject

Study the following sentence patterns:

The *harder* he works, **the** *better* his marks.
Je mehr er arbeitet, desto besser seine Noten.

When shall I come? — **The** *sooner* **the** *better*.
Wann soll ich kommen? – Je früher, desto besser.

How long is he going to stay? — **The** *longer* **the** *better*.
Wie lange wird er bleiben? – Je länger, desto lieber / besser.

The *longer* I know him, **the** *more* I like him.
Je länger ich ihn kenne, desto lieber mag ich ihn.

The *warmer* it is, **the** *worse* he feels.
Je wärmer es ist, desto schlechter fühlt er sich.

The *earlier* you leave now, **the** *sooner* you will be back again.
Je früher du jetzt gehst, desto früher wirst du wieder zurück sein.

The *more carefully* you write, **the** *nicer* your birthday card looks.
Je sorgfältiger du schreibst, desto netter sieht deine Geburtstagskarte aus.

Translate:

1. Je länger er warten musste, desto trauriger wurde er.
2. Je mehr sie darüber las, desto weniger verstand sie es.
3. Je schneller du arbeitest, desto früher wirst du fertig sein.
4. Je teurer die Jeans sind, desto besser passen sie.
5. Je weniger du schläfst, desto müder bist du.
6. Je mehr du rauchst, desto schlechter fühlst du dich.
7. Je mehr Make-up du verwendest, desto schlechter ist es für deine Haut.
8. Je lauter sie schrien, desto nervöser wurde sie.
9. Je unglücklicher sie ist, desto dicker wird sie.
10. Je schneller er läuft, desto erschöpfter ist er.
11. Je hilfreicher du bist, desto mehr Freunde wirst du haben.
12. Je länger sie zu Hause bei ihren Kindern bleibt, desto besser für sie.
13. Je schneller du isst, desto schlechter ist es für deinen Magen.
14. Je länger ich das Bild ansah, desto schöner schien es mir.
15. Je zorniger er wurde, desto mehr lachte ich.
16. Je wilder er tanzte, desto schlechter wurde ihr.
17. Je mehr er trank, desto schlimmer wurde sein Kopfweh.
18. Je schneller er fuhr, desto gefährlicher wurde es.
19. Je freundlicher der Arzt ist, desto mehr Patienten besuchen ihn.
20. Je sorgfältiger du lernst, desto leichter wird die Prüfung für dich sein.
21. Je eifersüchtiger du bist, desto schlimmer für eure Freundschaft.
22. Je gesünder du bist, desto glücklicher bist du.
23. Je mehr du liest, desto besser wirst du in Deutsch werden.
24. Je genauer du arbeitest, desto schöner wird dein Seidentuch sein.
25. Je mehr du fernsiehst, desto schlechter ist es für deine Augen.
26. Je frecher er ist, desto weniger mögen ihn die anderen Kinder.
27. Je öfter du dein Zimmer aufräumst, desto gemütlicher ist es.
28. Je schrecklicher der Film ist, desto mehr wirst du dich später fürchten.
29. Je schlechter seine Noten sind, desto mehr hasst er die Schule.
30. Je öfter du Flöte übst, desto besser kannst du spielen.
31. Je mehr Flecken auf deiner Hose sind, desto schmutziger sieht sie aus.
32. Je freundlicher du bist, desto lieber mögen dich die Menschen.
33. Je schöner das Wetter ist, desto fröhlicher sind die Menschen.
34. Je mehr Schokolade du isst, desto schlechter ist es für deine Zähne.
35. Je arroganter er ist, desto weniger Hilfe bekommt er.
36. Je öfter dein Bleistift auf den Boden fällt, desto öfter bricht er.
37. Je größer die Wohnung ist, desto besser für die Kinder.
38. Je mehr Blumen im Garten wachsen, desto netter sieht er aus.
39. Je mehr Sorgen du dir machst, desto schlechter ist es für deine Gesundheit.

HOW TO TRANSLATE „WERDEN"

1. TO BE

I want to **be** a teacher when I grow up.	*Ich möchte Lehrer werden, wenn ich groß bin.*
He **is** always first.	*Er wird immer Erster.*
He **was** second.	*Er wurde Zweiter.*
What's that going to **be**?	*Was soll das werden?*
It **is** time we **went**. Achtung: Nach *it is time* steht **Past tense**!	*Es **wird** Zeit, dass wir gehen.*
It will **be** all right.	*Es wird schon werden.*
There must **be** a change.	*Es muss anders werden.*

2. TO BECOME   für *langsameres* WERDEN

He will **become** a teacher.	*Er wird Lehrer werden.*
He has **become** a famous man.	*Er ist ein berühmter Mann geworden.*
What's to **become** of him?	*Was soll aus ihm werden?*
It is **becoming** warmer.	*Es wird wärmer.*
What will **become** of the children?	*Was wird/soll aus den Kindern werden?*
What has **become** of him?	*Was ist aus ihm geworden?*

„become" is often used with the following adjectives:
warm, dark, harder, difficult, nice, interested, expensive, angry ...

3. TO GET   für *langsameres* WERDEN

I am **getting** cold.		*Mir wird kalt.*		
We are **getting** ready.		*Wie werden fertig.*		
She **got** well again.		*Sie wurde wieder gesund.*		
It is **getting**	cold.	*Es wird*	*kalt.*	
	dark.		*dunkel.*	
	late.		*spät.*	
	better.		*besser.*	
	worse.		*schlechter.*	
He is **getting**	old.	*Er wird*	*alt.*	
	tired.		*müde.*	
	paid.		*bezahlt.*	
	excited.		*aufgeregt.*	
	nervous.		*nervös.*	
	wet.		*nass.*	
	drunk.		*betrunken.*	
	angry.		*zornig.*	

4. TO GO

to **go**	crazy	*verrückt werden*	
	blind	*blind*	
	red	*rot*	
	sour	*sauer*	
	pale	*blass*	

5. TO GROW   für *langsameres* WERDEN

to **grow**	angry	*zornig werden*
	old	*alt*

6. TO TURN

to **turn**	pale	*blass werden*
	sour	*sauer*
	cold	*kalt*
	grey	*grau*
	white	*weiß*
	red	*rot*
	fifteen	*fünfzehn*
	Muslim	*Muslim / Moslem*
	Catholic	*katholisch*
	traitor	*Verräter*
	to stone	*zu Stein werden*
	to gold	*zu Gold*
	to dust	*zu Staub*

His hair has **turned** white overnight. — *Sein Haar ist über Nacht weiß geworden.*

The milk has **turned** sour. — *Die Milch ist sauer geworden.*

She **turned** pale and fainted. — *Sie wurde blass und fiel in Ohnmacht.*

The leaves are beginning to **turn** brown. — *Die Blätter beginnen braun zu werden.*

The meat **turned** bad. — *Das Fleisch wurde schlecht.*

He has just **turned** twenty. — *Er ist gerade zwanzig geworden.*

It will **turn out** all right. — *Es wird schon wieder gut werden.*

The meal is going to **turn out** nicely. — *Das Essen wird bestimmt gut werden.*

The old books **turned to** dust. — *Die alten Bücher wurden zu Staub.*

The cigarette smoke **turned** the curtains yellow. — *Der Zigarettenrauch ließ die Vorhänge gelb werden.*

7. TO COME

He **came** first.	*Er wurde Erster.*
Nothing will **come of** it. That won't **come to** anything.	*Daraus wird nichts werden.*
It has **come to** nothing.	*Daraus ist nichts geworden.*
The photos have **come out** nicely.	*Die Fotos sind gut geworden.*
It'll **come out** okay.	*Es wird schon werden.*
Winter is **coming**.	*Es wird Winter.*

8. OTHER EXPRESSIONS

It's bound to be a girl.	*Es wird sicher ein Mädchen werden.*
My / Your day will come.	*Was nicht ist, kann noch werden.*
What's going to happen now?	*Was soll nun werden?*
I **feel sick**.	*Mir wird schlecht.*

COMPARISON: ... and ...   *immer ...*

Study the following sentence patterns:

His behaviour is getting **better and better**.
*Sein Benehmen wird **immer besser**.*

Her marks are getting **worse and worse**.
*Ihre Noten werden **immer schlechter**.*

The pond is getting **fuller and fuller** because it is raining heavily.
*Der Teich wird **immer voller**, weil es stark regnet.*

He ran **faster and faster**. / He ran **more and more quickly**.
*Er rannte **immer schneller**.*

He calls her **more and more often**.
*Er ruft sie **immer öfter** an.*

The book is getting **more and more interesting** towards the end.
*Das Buch wird dem Ende zu **immer interessanter**.*

The film is getting **more and more thrilling**. I warn you!
*Der Film wird **immer spannender**. Ich warne dich!*

He is working **more and more carefully**.
*Er arbeitet **immer sorgfältiger**.*

Maths is getting **more and more difficult**.
*Mathematik wird **immer schwieriger**.*

Cigarettes are getting **more and more expensive**.
*Zigaretten werden **immer teurer**.*

Peter thinks it is becoming **more and more difficult** to find a nice wife.
*Peter denkt, es wird **immer schwieriger**, eine nette Ehefrau zu finden.*

Computers cost **less and less** money.
*Computer kosten **immer weniger**.*

Before doing the following exercise study pages 54 to 58 carefully!

Bevor du diese Übung machst, studiere die Seiten 54 bis 58 sorgfältig!

Translate:
1. Heutzutage lernen immer mehr Kinder Französisch und Spanisch.
2. Jim findet Tennis immer weniger interessant.
3. Er kann immer höher springen.
4. Die Gäste sangen immer lauter.
5. Anna isst immer weniger.
6. Tom isst immer weniger Süßigkeiten.
7. Wie steht's mit deinem Kopfweh? – Es wird immer besser.
8. Es wird immer schwieriger, einen guten Freund zu finden, meint Lucy.
9. Tom interessiert sich immer mehr für Computer.
10. Das Wetter wird immer kälter.
11. Seine Gesundheit wird immer schlechter.
12. Er traf sie immer öfter.
13. Es wird immer finsterer. Ich denke, wir sollten jetzt gehen.
14. Bill mochte Mandy immer lieber.
15. Peter arbeitet immer eifriger.
16. Es wird immer später und wir sind noch immer hier!
17. Mein Fuß schmerzte immer stärker.
18. Sein Vater trank immer mehr.
19. Herr Miller beklagt sich, dass die Kinder immer frecher werden.
20. Seine Probleme werden immer größer.
21. Seine Freundinnen werden immer jünger je älter er wird.
22. Die Schreie wurden immer lauter.
23. Die Armen werden immer ärmer, die Reichen immer reicher.
24. Die alten Hits werden immer beliebter.
25. Die Preise für Bananen werden immer höher.
26. Er versprach ihr immer mehr, aber sie verließ ihn dennoch.
27. Sie kommt immer später nach Hause.
28. Ihr Gesicht wurde immer blässer.
29. Mir wird immer kälter.
30. Sie wurde immer verrückter.
31. Herr Smith wurde immer zorniger.
32. Es wird immer teurer ins Ausland zu fahren.
33. Mutter wird immer nervöser.
34. Wir werden immer älter und weiser.
35. Sie wurde immer röter im Gesicht.
36. Frau Austin wurde immer blinder.

PAST PERFECT TENSE SIMPLE

1. Formation: *had + past participle*

Examples:
I *had done*
she *had seen*
we *had been*
they *had come*

2. Use:

We use the *past perfect tense* to express that something *had happened / had been done* before something else happened / was done.
The anteriority is stressed.

(*Wir verwenden die past perfect tense, um auszudrücken, dass etwas geschehen war oder getan worden war, bevor etwas anderes geschah / getan wurde. Die Vorzeitigkeit wird betont.*)

Study the following examples:
I **had** *already* **finished** my work when he asked me to go out with him.
Ich hatte meine Arbeit gerade fertig, als er mich bat, mit ihm auszugehen.
After Mr Berger **had worked** all day, he fell asleep.
Nachdem Herr Berger den ganzen Tag gearbeitet hatte, schlief er ein.
When Linda arrived home, Frank **had** *already* **left**.
After he **had had** a rich meal, he felt tired.
Before she went to town, she **had cleaned** her house carefully.
I lost my new umbrella shortly *after* I **had bought** it.
When he got out of the bus, he saw that he **had lost** his money.
After he **had found** his book again, he began to read.
I **had** *just* **entered** the room when the telephone rang.
Before he left the shopping centre, he **had spent** all his money.
Mary told me his name *after* he **had left**.
After I **had slept**, I felt fresh and relaxed.

Keep in mind:	after + past perfect tense	⇨	past tense
	before + past tense	⇨	past perfect tense

PAST PERFECT OR PAST TENSE

1. After I .... (see) the horror film I .... (be) terribly afraid.
2. Each time before Tom .... (go) on a journey, he .... (be) rather nervous and exhausted.
3. After my cleaning woman .... (leave), my house .... (be) clean and tidy.
4. When Mr Miller .... (watch) Miss Smith closely, he .... (give) her the job.
5. After we .... (have) dinner, we .... (go) for a walk.
6. After he .... (read) about the murder in the newspaper, he .... (call) the police.
7. I .... (not / can) walk because I .... (break) my leg on my way home.
8. We .... (reach) the house one minute before the storm .... (begin).
9. Sue .... (go) to bed as soon as she .... (finish) reading the book.
10. As the milk .... (turn) she .... (not / can) bake a cake.
11. After Pam .... (hide) her diary, she .... (not / can) find it any more.
12. As Tom's watch .... (be) slow, he .... (miss) the train.
13. Oliver .... (be) very angry because all the others .... (laugh) at him.
14. When the Robins .... (pack) their suitcases, they .... (call) a taxi and .... (go) to the airport.
15. She .... (hurry) home again as soon as she .... (do) her shopping.
16. After he .... (eat) all the sandwiches, he .... (drink) one bottle of lemonade.
17. He .... (work) in private industry before he .... (become) a teacher.
18. As I .... (miss) the last bus, I .... (must) walk to town.
19. He .... (take) his dog for a walk as soon as he .... (do) his housework.

20. We .... (be) tired because we .... (work) a lot.
21. Mrs Lincoln .... (live) in England before she .... (emigrate) to America.
22. When he .... (leave), he .... (see) that he .... (forget) his purse.
23. He .... (begin) to weep after he .... (read) the letter.
24. The old woman .... (already die) when the doctor .... (arrive).
25. When she .... (enter), she .... (find) a message that her friend .... (already leave).
26. After the opera singer .... (sing) the song, the audience .... (applaud).
27. I .... (feel) fresh and happy after I .... (sleep).
28. After he .... (shout) at me, he .... (be) very sorry.
29. The pupils .... (see) the film after they .... (read) the book.
30. When he .... (arrive) at the station, the train .... (already leave).
31. I .... (not watch) the film because I .... (see) it the night before.
32. When they .... (get) to the stadium, the soccer match .... (already start).
33. When she .... (come) home she .... (notice) that somebody .... (steal) her ring from the shelf.
34. When she .... (hear) the scream she .... (know) that something terrible .... (happen).
35. She .... (pass) the exam easily because she .... (work) a lot.
36. He .... (know) that he .... (see) her somewhere before.
37. After Bob .... (be) to the cinema, he .... (do) his homework.
38. They .... (be) poor after they .... (waste) all their money.

39. Sarah .... (tell) me lots of incredible things after he .... (leave).
40. He .... (tell) me his name after I .... (ask) him.
41. I .... (not / can) write the letter because I .... (lose) my pen somewhere.
42. After she .... (write) the letter to Peter, she .... (buy) a stamp, ... (run) to town and .... (post) it.
43. The storm .... (break) the kitchen window before we .... (can) shut it.
44. After Frank .... (recognise) Linda, he .... (run) as fast as he .... (can) to catch her.
45. As Laura .... (lose) her wonderful diamond ring, she .... (be) totally desperate.
46. As he .... (never / meet) his uncle from America, he .... (not / recognise) him at the airport.
47. Tom .... (not / be) thirsty. He .... (just / have) a glass of lemonade.
48. We .... (want) to invite our neighbours to dinner, but they .... (not / can) come because they .... (already / buy) tickets for the opera.
49. I .... (not / get) any slice of cake because they .... (eat up) everything.
50. She .... (be) very grateful for what I .... (do) for her.
51. The burglar .... (not / want) to admit that he .... (break) into the house.
52. He .... (want) to know why we .... (leave) so early.
53. He .... (smoke) a big cigar after we .... (finish) lunch.
54. As his suitcase .... (disappear), he .... (must) borrow his friend's pyjamas.
55. I .... (just close) the door when the storm .... (set) in.
56. Before I .... (can) warn him he .... (already / slip) on the banana skin.

PAST PERFECT TENSE AND MODAL VERBS

CAN	I **had been able to** solve the riddle before he came.
CANNOT	He **had not been able to / hadn't been able to / had been unable to** finish the letter before she arrived.
MAY	After I **had been allowed to** leave hospital, I went home.
MUST NOT	After she **hadn't been allowed to** see the horror film, she was terribly angry.
MUST	After he **had had to help** mother the whole afternoon, he was tired.
NEEDN'T	He told me that he **hadn't had** to water the flowers.

1. After they .... (may) see the film, they .... (must) write an essay about it.
2. Ben .... (cannot) tell the joke before the teacher came in.
3. After she .... (must) study a lot, she .... (can) pass her test easily.
4. After Tom .... (may) play in the garden, he .... (must) do his homework.
5. They went to the cinema after they .... (can) repair Peter's bike.
6. After Bill .... (must not) go to the party because of his bad marks, he cried.
7. As he .... (needn't) take care of his little sister, he went to see his friend Rick.
8. They .... (already can) climb the mountain three times, when they tried again.
9. After he .... (must) stay in bed for three weeks, he felt very weak when he got up again.

CONDITIONAL III

Conditional I, II see ☺ III p 6–13

Conditional III is used to express **impossibility**.
(*um eine Unmöglichkeit auszudrücken*)

1. **Impossibility** with result **in the present**:
   (*Unmöglichkeit mit Resultat in der Gegenwart*)

if + past perfect	⇨	would + verb
		'd + verb
		could + verb

   Examples:
   If he *had not hurried* like this, he **'d not be** out of breath <u>now</u>.
   If he *had listened to* her, he **would not be** in trouble <u>now</u>.
   If she *had saved* more money, she **could buy** a new car <u>this year</u>.
   If he *hadn't sold* his car, he **wouldn't have to walk** <u>now</u>.
   If she *hadn't drunk* too much wine, she **wouldn't be** sick <u>today</u>.

2. **Impossibility** with result **in the past**:
   (*Unmöglichkeit mit Resultat in der Vergangenheit*)

if + past perfect	⇨	would have + past participle *(3. Verbform)*
		'd have + past participle
		could have + past participle

   Examples:
   If we *had hurried* a bit more, we **would have met** them at the airport.
   If Roger *hadn't come* to my party, it **would have been** less fun.
   If he *had been* thirsty, he **would have had** some tea.
   You **would have seen** Lucy *if* you *had gone* to the disco last night.
   I **would not have missed** the date *if* I *hadn't been* ill.

CONDITIONAL I, II, III

1. If breakfast isn't ready, I .... (go) without it.
2. If I had known that he needed me, I .... (help) him.
3. If Ben dances with Linda, I swear you, I .... (run) away from the party.
4. If Robert tried again, he .... (succeed).
5. If you leave milk in the sun, it .... (turn) sour.
6. He would get better marks if he .... (not / be) so lazy.
7. If you hurry a bit, you .... (catch) the train.
8. If it stopped raining, we .... (can) go for a walk now.
9. If Peter had seen her, he .... (ask) her.
10. If Sue calls Tom a pest, he .... (get) angry.
11. You must tell me if you .... (be) in trouble.
12. Bill would have bought a new car if he .... (have) enough money.
13. You .... (can) phone me if you need any help.
14. If mum .... (be) here, I could ask her about the recipe.
15. If Pit doesn't like his job, he .... (must) change it.
16. If he had offered me the ticket, I .... (take) it.
17. If you are in a hurry, you .... (can) take my bike.
18. If I knew how I could help him, I .... (help).
19. If you had given him my telephone number, it .... (be) a great help.
20. If you drop a thin glass on the stone floor, it .... (break).
21. It would be very nice of you if you .... (go) to see him.
22. If you don't touch the dog, it .... (not / bite) you.
23. If you tease my cat, it .... (scratch) you.
24. We could have tea together if she .... (be) at home.
25. If we had stayed longer, we .... (meet) her.
26. If he returns, you .... (must) tell me, please.
27. If he had run a bit faster, he .... (be) here now.
28. The thief would have taken her money if she .... (not / have) a spray can.
29. If they hadn't searched for the little girl, she .... (freeze) to death.
30. If you put a glass over a burning candle, the flame .... (smother).
31. If he had saved some money, he .... (can) buy a flat now.

32. If they arrive late, you .... (must) inform me.
33. Tom would never have caught that terrible cold if he .... (put) on his jacket and his cap.
34. If you touch a bee, it .... (sting) you.
35. If I had known that he was such a pest, I .... (not / invite) him.
36. I .... (go) and call him if you need him now.
37. I won't tell you anything unless you .... (can) keep a secret.
38. If he hadn't spent all his money, he .... (can / buy) a new motorbike last year.
39. If she hadn't won in the lottery, she .... (not have) such a nice house now.
40. If she had green hair, they .... (laugh) at her.
41. If it is stormy, we .... (not / can) go for a sail.
42. She would not have stayed alive if the doctor .... (not / come) in time.
43. If Rose had invited him, he .... (be) at her place now.
44. He .... (not / can / pass) his exams if she hadn't studied with him.
45. If he .... (look) at me, I would have gone red.
46. If he came, I .... (be) happy.
47. He'd never have asked her to marry him if he .... (know) about her past.
48. If the wine-grower comes, ... (tell) him to leave twenty bottles, please.
49. If you drink too much coffee, your blood pressure .... (get) higher.
50. If it had been very late at night, we .... (walk) her home.
51. It would be a great idea if we .... (go) to the concert tonight.
52. If he wears his new leather boots, he .... (always / feel) very cool.
53. If you drink two pints of beer, you .... (have) too much alcohol in your blood to be allowed to drive.
54. He would never leave the house if the sun .... (not / shine) today.
55. She .... (not / stay) if he hadn't asked her.
56. If I find your key, I .... (phone) you at once.

57. If I .... (know) earlier, I would have sent a telegram at once.
58. If I hadn't eaten so much, I .... (not / be) so sleepy now.
59. If I say "yes" now, you .... (say) "no"!
60. If I .... (stay up) late last night, I would be tired now.
61. If he doesn't turn up, we .... (go) without him.
62. If I prepare some tea, ... (you / have) a cup with me?
63. Would he marry her if she .... (not / be) so rich?
64. What will you do if you .... (not / find) your key?
65. I'm sure that if you apologize, he .... (forgive) you.
66. If you brake on ice, your car .... (skid).
67. If he had left a message on the table, she .... (know) where he is now.
68. What would Sarah do if she .... (fail) in her driving test?
69. If a dog is happy and peaceful, it .... (wag) its tail.
70. If I could leave my suitcase here, I .... (be) very pleased.
71. If she had had her leg in plaster, she .... (cannot) go skiing with us last year.
72. If a chameleon wants to hide, it .... (change) its colour.
73. If she .... (keep) a diary, she would be able to write about her problems.
74. If a hedgehog is afraid, it .... (roll) itself up into a ball.
75. If I were Bob, I .... (not / go) to Lisa's party.
76. If they put salt on the icy roads, the ice .... (melt).
77. If I had known his name, I .... (not / ask).
78. If we had booked seats earlier, we .... (sit) in the front row now.
79. She .... (not / have to) spend her holidays in a summer college if she had passed her final exams.
80. If you send light through a prism, you .... (see) the rainbow colours.
81. She .... (soon feel) all right again if she takes this medicine.
82. If a meteor enters the atmosphere, it .... (begin) to glow.

REPORTED SPEECH

1. When the **reporting verb** *(Zeitwort des Sagens: say, tell, remark, explain ...)* is in

present		
present perfect	⇨	NO CHANGE OF TENSES
future		

   Examples:

   Peter **says**, "The train **is** late."
   Peter **says** that the train **is** late.

   She **says**, "*I* **have** never **eaten** spinach."
   She **says** that *she* **has** never **eaten** spinach.

   He **has remarked** recently, "*I* **will try** again."
   He **has remarked** recently that *he* **will try** again.

   Dad **will say**, "*You* **painted** the fence perfectly!"
   Dad **will say** that *I / you* **painted** the fence perfectly.

2. When the **reporting verb** *(Zeitwort des Sagens: say, tell, remark, explain ...)* is in

past tense	⇨	CHANGE OF TENSES
present tense	⇨	past tense
past tense	⇨	past perfect tense
present perfect tense	⇨	past perfect tense
past perfect tense	⇨	past perfect tense
future	⇨	conditional: would + verb

   Examples:

   He **explained**, "*I* **don't eat** much meat."
   He **explained** that *he* **didn't eat** much meat.

Sarah **said**, "*He* **was** really charming."
Sarah **said** that *he* **had been** really charming.

He **said**, "*I* **have** never **met** a lovelier girl before."
He **was sure** that *he* **had** never **met** a lovelier girl before.

She **told** us, "*I* **was** at the zoo for the first time and *I* **had** never **seen** a real tiger before."
She **told** us that *she* **had been** at the zoo for the first time and that *she* **had** never **seen** a real tiger before.

He **said**, "*I* **am going to** invite her for dinner."
He **said** that *he* **was going to** invite her for dinner.

She **thought**, "*I* **will have** a cup of tea."
She **thought** that *she* **would have** a cup of tea.

3. The following verbs **do not** normally **change**:
(*Folgende Verben verändern sich normalerweise nicht.*)

> **would**
> **should**
> **ought to**   ⇨   **NO CHANGE**
> **mustn't**
> **might**
> **had better** (*lieber sollen*)

	↗	**could / was, were able to**	
could	⇨	**could / had been able to**	
	↘	**could / would be able to**	(for future)
	↗	**must**	
must	⇨	**must / had to**	
	↘	**must / would have to**	(for future)

Examples:

He **said**, "*I* **would** like to see *this* film."
He **said** that *he* **would** like to see *that* film.

She **said**, "*We* **should** go home *now*."
She **said** that *we / they* **should** go home *then*.

Frank **remarked**, "*I* **ought to** call her."
Frank **remarked** that *he* **ought to** call her.

Father **said**, "*You* **mustn't** leave *your* toys on the floor."
Father **said** that *we* **mustn't** leave *our* toys on the floor.

Mum **said**, "*I* **might** be a bit late."
Mum **said** that *she* **might** be a bit late.

Ann **said**, "*We* **had better** leave *now*." (*Wir sollten lieber jetzt gehen.*)
Ann **said** that *they / we* **had better** leave *then*.

He **said**, "*You* **had better** warm up *your* muscles before *you* **step** on *your* snowboard."
He **said** that *I* **had better** warm up *my* muscles before *I* **stepped** on *my* snowboard.

He **said**, "*I* **could not** come on Friday."
He **said** that *he* **could not / was not able to / had not been able to** come on Friday.

He **said**, "*I* **could** come at five *tomorrow*."
He **said** that *he* **could** come / **would be able to** come at five *the next day*.

He **said**, "*I* **must** go *now*."
He **said** that *he* **must** go / **had to** go *then*.

"*We* **must** paint the fence *tomorrow*," he **said**.
He **said** that *they / we* **must / would have to** paint the fence *the next day*.

He **told** us, "*We* **must** leave early *tomorrow* if *we* **don't** want to miss the plane."
He **told** us that *we* **must / would have to** leave early *the next day* if *we* **didn't** want to miss the plane.

4. Conditional II sentences DO NOT CHANGE

Examples:

He **said**, "If *I* **were** healthier, *I* **would** go skiing."
He **said** that *if* he **were** healthier, *he* **would** go skiing.

She **told** us, "*I* **would** help *you* if *I* **could**."
She **told** us that *she* **would** help *us* if *she* **could**.

5. If you report **facts,** there is NO CHANGE OF TENSES

Examples:

She **said**, "The Seine **flows** through Paris." (Fact, true)
She **said** that the Seine **flows** through Paris.

The teacher **said**, "The earth **turns** around the sun." (Fact, true)
The teacher **said** that the earth **turns** around the sun.

She **explained**, "Rome **is** the capital of Italy." (Fact, true)
She **explained** that Rome **is** the capital of Italy.

6. OTHER CHANGES:

I, we, my, our	⇨	**third person**
here	⇨	**there**
now	⇨	**then**
this / these	⇨	**that / those**
today	⇨	**that day**
tonight	⇨	**that night**
yesterday	⇨	**the day before**
the day before yesterday	⇨	**two days before**
tomorrow	⇨	**the next / the following day**
the day after tomorrow	⇨	**in two days' time**
last week / month / year	⇨	**the previous week / month / year**
a year ago	⇨	**a year before / the previous year**
next week / month / year	⇨	**the following week / month / year**

Attention 1: **Personal pronouns** and **possessive adjectives** are
not changed if the **speaker** reports **his own words**.
(*Die **Personalpronomen** und **besitzanzeigenden Adjektive** werden
nicht verändert, wenn **der Sprecher selbst seine eigenen Worte
wiederholt**.*)

Example:
I said, "I will invite Joe for dinner to **my** house."
I said that **I** would invite Joe for dinner to **my** house.

Attention 2: To avoid ambiguity the **person must be mentioned**.
(*Um Missverständnisse zu vermeiden, muss die **Person erwähnt werden**.*)

Example:

- Correct: **He** said, "**He** climbed over the fence."
  He said that **the man / the burglar / the boy** had climbed over the fence.
- Wrong: **He** said that **he** had climbed over the fence.
  (*Das würde bedeuten, dass **er selbst** über den Zaun geklettert ist!*)

Attention 3: **No change** of time expressions if you report the same day.
(*Keine Veränderung der Zeitausdrücke, **wenn am selben Tag** berichtet wird.*)

Example:
Rita said, "He brought me the parcel **yesterday**."
Rita said **this morning** that he had brought her the parcel **yesterday**.
(**not:** the day before)

> **7.** In **spoken** English there is sometimes **no change of tenses**.
> (*Im **gesprochenen** Englisch werden die **Zeiten oft nicht verwandelt**.*)

Example:

Mum:	"Where's Tony?"
I:	"He's up in his room doing his homework."
Dad:	"What did mum want to know?"
I:	"She just **wanted** to know where Tony **is** and I **told** her that he **is** up in his room doing his homework."
Dad:	"Thanks!"

PUT INTO REPORTED SPEECH

1. The speaker announces, "The six o'clock train will be late."
2. Mark said to me, "Paris was wonderful and exciting."
3. Mr Miller said, "The people are waiting outside."
4. Paul complained, "Susan doesn't like jazz."
5. Mum will say, "I have been working all the time."
6. She told us, "I don't smoke and I am not very fond of beer and wine."
7. Liz said, "I can't come to your party. I must take care of little Ben."
8. He remarked, "I have never seen a more thrilling film."
9. She said, "I'm going to spend my weekend in the mountains."
10. He thought, "I'll have a cup of coffee now."
11. He said, "Peter would like to have a party at the weekend."
12. Sally said, "We should leave now. It is late."
13. She said, "We had better tell her the truth now."
14. They feared, "We might be late."
15. Bill told me, "I could not send her any flowers because the flower shop was closed."
16. Father said, "We must repair the fence next summer."
17. Tom said, "If I had more time, I would go to the concert on Friday."
18. Father is sure, "The train will arrive at one, so there is plenty of time."
19. He said, "We ought to send her birthday greetings."
20. I told them, "I will have a garden party for all my friends in the summer holidays."
21. He told us, "He showed me more than one thousand photos in one night."
22. Linda was so happy, "Sam was so nice and friendly. He even helped me carry my bags."
23. She told us, "Next week I'm flying to London and I'm going to visit the British Museum."
24. He said, "I've been waiting for two hours but she hasn't turned up."
25. Mother said, "It's time to leave."
26. Uncle Bill told us, "I returned yesterday. It was really wonderful. I'm totally relaxed."
27. The teacher told us, "The dinosaurs died out because of a change in the climate."
28. Tony said, "If we had maps, we could find the right direction."
29. Phil said, "Ben is trying to breed mice and then he wants to sell them."
30. Sue explained, "I can't stay in the sun for a long time and I don't like a hot climate."
31. The doctor told me, "Too much sun is not healthy for your skin."
32. The experts hope, "One day we will find something against the virus."

33. Peter told me, "In the horror film lots of gigantic spiders escaped from a laboratory and spread all over the town. It was awful and I couldn't sleep well after seeing the film."
34. He told me, "I could see the star with the naked eye because the night was so clear."
35. The speaker said, "Shortly before the earthquake the inhabitants could hear a kind of thunder."
36. Mary told us, "I've got an allergy to strawberries."
37. Frank told us, "Sally's story is quite unbelievable. I know her husband very well and I can't believe that he really shouted at her."
38. Mother said to me, "Your complaint is really ridiculous."
39. He was sure, "If I lived in Vienna, I would go to the opera as often as possible."
40. Tina is only four, but she said, "The earth is smaller than the sun."
41. The scientist said, "We are trying to find out more about the deadly virus."
42. Fred complained, "Lucy spends too much money. Yesterday she bought two new coats. I don't know what to do with her."
43. Mother warned me, "You had better take an umbrella, it might rain soon."
44. She told us, "I was in India twice and I had some really shocking experiences there."
45. She said, "I didn't quite understand."
46. Sue is sure, "I'll soon be able to speak French very well."
47. Frank said to me, "If I were you, I wouldn't spend such a lot of money on clothes."
48. Father told us, "Every day I listened to the radio until midnight and then I went to bed."
49. He said, "I don't know why he was so unfriendly to me."
50. The teacher said, "At the North Pole the sun never sets in summer."
51. He said, "I can't come tonight, because I must finish my book report for school, but I could come round at five tomorrow."
52. Our American guests say, "Austria is a very beautiful country to live in."
53. Tom told us, "I ran very fast, but he caught me at the corner and threw a big snowball into my face."
54. Mr Miller was surprised, "Most Austrian children speak English pretty well and they understood everything I said."
55. She said, "I have no time to cook the meal now and I'll be late tonight. Tony phoned me and asked me to help him translate a letter."
56. Father came in and said, "You mustn't watch such a stupid film."
57. Mother announced, "I'll go to town this afternoon. If you need anything, I'll get it for you."

58. She wrote, "We've been having a wonderful weekend in the Tyrol."
59. Michael answered, "You will soon know that you are wrong but then it'll be too late."
60. He told me, "I have never been to Paris. I would like to spend my next holidays there."
61. She said, "I don't want another pet. I want to keep my cat."
62. She wrote to me, "I will arrive at five on Monday and I would be very glad if you picked me up at the station."
63. He said, "Three years ago I was in Vienna visiting all the famous sights and galleries. I was really impressed and I'm going to come again with my family this year."
64. Dad said, "If the weather is fine tomorrow, we'll make a trip to a lake."
65. Mother warned me, "You mustn't play the trumpet now because it's too late and the neighbours will complain if you make such a noise."
66. Mandy told me, "You needn't help me with the homework. I have already had a look at it and it isn't difficult at all."
67. Father said, "I am very sorry, but this is my last word and I don't want to talk about it again and again."
68. Mrs Smith was happy, "I am feeling a lot better today. It's good to be back home from hospital."
69. He told the reporter, "I went into the cave with some friends. We were looking for minerals. It was rather slippery and Pit fell over a stone. He lost his torch and we had to find our way back without any light. It took us nearly eight hours to get back to the daylight."
70. Judy was sure, "I will never run away from home any more because my parents had two horrible days and I don't want to hurt them a second time."
71. Pit phoned me and said, "I can't play tennis with you today because I've hurt my knee."
72. Charlie said, "I can't believe it's true that she left him. He was such a nice man and he loved her so much."
73. Mr Winner told us, "I've never seen a real tiger before."
74. Sally wrote, "I had to go to New York last week and I almost missed the plane."
75. Mother told me, "You can't wear those orange trousers today. You know uncle Bill is very conservative."
76. We told Tom, "You must learn to get rid of your aggressiveness in a different way."
77. Mr Stone told us, "I was in my office. Suddenly I had a strange phone call. It was a man who had died two years ago."
78. She said, "I'm a very careful driver so you needn't be scared."
79. He said, "We ought to tidy the house before our parents come back."

80. She said, "We were thinking of selling our old car but we've decided to keep it for one more year."
81. Peter told his friend, "If Sally weren't so jealous, I would ask her to marry me."
82. She said to her, "I must speak to you after you've finished your work."
83. After the expedition he said, "The most important thing in all the dangers was never to give up hope."
84. She was sure, "You can do it if you only try."
85. He said, "You may see my holiday photos if you like."
86. Tom said, "I like my dolls better than Susan's racing cars."
87. Linda was happy, "Rick is going to spend the weekend with us. He's flying home earlier than he expected."
88. Our teacher explained, "In the Antarctic there is perpetual ice."
89. John confessed, "I've been smoking too much that's why I've got a bad cough."
90. She explained, "Nancy's husband is the man over there. The one who is talking to Mrs Notbush."
91. He was sure, "They will be here soon. We are going to have a great party."
92. He promised, "I'll come as soon as I can, but you needn't wait for me."
93. The policeman explained, "You mustn't cross the street here."
94. She mentioned, "I would not do this if I were in your place."
95. She said, "You must decide for yourself what you are going to do."
96. He promised, "When I come round the day after tomorrow, I'll bring you the book I borrowed from you last week. I won't forget it."
97. She says to him, "I can't live with you any longer. We are too different."
98. He told us, "Lucy might have to stay in bed for two weeks. She has got the flu. So we must start without her."
99. The speaker said, "All spectators should keep their tickets till the end of the match."
100. Einstein said, "Mass is relative."
101. Peter complained, "I've been waiting for her call for three hours."
102. Mary is happy, "I've finished this difficult exercise."
103. He was sure, "I last saw her five weeks ago."
104. She said, "The Danube flows through Vienna."
105. Mary told us, "If Brian came to my party, I would be surprised."
106. He informed us, "You needn't stay any longer if you don't like."
107. He will say to me, "You must be back at ten."
108. He has told us recently, "I will try to get some new stamps for your collection when I'm in Vienna."
109. She said, "If I am late, you must put the lunch into the microwave."
110. Father said to me, "You may watch TV if there is a good film on."

RELATIVE PRONOUNS: WHO, WHICH, THAT, WHAT

> **1. Relative pronouns for persons:**
>
> | | | |
> |---|---|---|
> | who / that | nominative | (1. Fall) |
> | whose | possessive | (2. Fall) |
> | to / for / with ... who**m** | with prepositions | |
> | who / that ... to / for / with | with prepositions | |
> | who / whom / that | accusative | (4. Fall) |

1. Fall:

The man **who / that** lives next door is Mr Lincoln. *(Der Mann **der / welcher** ...)*

The woman **who / that** asked you is Mrs Smith. *(Die Frau **die / welche** ...)*

The boy **who / that** gave you the flower is Bill Barns. *(Der Bub **der / welcher** ...)*

2. Fall:

This is the girl **whose** parents went to Australia. *(... **dessen** Eltern ...)*

The boy **whose** cat died is very sad. *(... **dessen** Katze ...)*

This is the woman **whose** son is in America now. *(... **deren** Sohn ...)*

With prepositions:

The man **to whom** you spoke is Mick's teacher. *(... **mit dem** ...) (written)*

The man **who / that** you spoke **to** is Mick's teacher. *(spoken English)*

Anmerkung: Im **gesprochenen, modernen** Englisch ziehen wir die Form

                who .... to / for / with vor. Beachte die Satzstellung!

                In diesen Fällen kann das Relativpronomen **entfallen**!

                Vor who / that darf **keine Präposition** stehen.

The man you spoke **to** is Mick's teacher. *(spoken)*

The girl **with whom** I saw Peter is his new friend. *(... **mit der** ...) (written)*

The girl **who / that** I saw Peter **with** is his new friend. *(Satzstellung!) (spoken)*

The girl I saw Peter **with** is his new friend. *(Relativpronomen entfällt) (spoken)*

This is the old woman **for whom** my mother cooks. *(... **für die** ...) (written)*

This is the old woman **who / that** my mother cooks **for**. *(spoken English)*

This is the old woman my mother cooks **for**. *(Relativpronomen entfällt) (spoken)*

The man **about whom** I told you is Sue's uncle. *(... **über den** ...) (written English)*

The man **who / that** I told you **about** is Sue's uncle. *(spoken English)*

The man I told you **about** is Sue's uncle. *(Relativpronomen entfällt) (spoken)*

4. Fall:

The man **whom** we met is Mr Smith. *(... **den** / **welchen** ...) (written English)*
The man **who / that** we met is Mr Smith. *(spoken English)*
The man we met is Mr Smith. *(Relativpronomen entfällt) (spoken English)*
*Anmerkung: Auch im 4. Fall kann das Relativpronomen **entfallen**.*

This is the girl **whom** he loves so much. *(written English)*
This is the girl **who / that** he loves so much. *(spoken English)*
This is the girl he loves so much. *(Relativpronomen entfällt) (spoken English)*

> **2. Relative pronouns for <u>animals and things</u>:**
>
> | | | |
> |---|---|---|
> | which / that | nominative | (1. Fall) |
> | whose | possessive | (2. Fall) |
> | to / for / with ... which | with prepositions | |
> | which / that ... to / for / with | with prepositions | |
> | which / that | accusative | (4. Fall) |

1. Fall:

This is the dog **which / that** bit Robert. *(... **der** / **welcher** ...)*
The book **which / that** is lying on the table is Bill's. *(... **das** / **welches** ...)*

2. Fall:

The book **whose** cover is dirty belongs to Simon. *(... **dessen** ...)*
The car **whose** windscreen is broken is my father's. *(... **dessen** ...)*

With prepositions:
The cat **to which** you gave the milk is Lucy's cat. *(... **der** / **welcher** ...) (written)*
The cat **which / that** you gave the milk **to** is Lucy's cat. *(Satzstellung!) (spoken)*
The cat you gave the milk **to** is Lucy's cat. *(Relativpronomen entfällt) (spoken)*

The book **for which** you are looking is on the kitchen table. *(**das/welches**) (written)*
The book **which / that** you are looking **for** is on the kitchen table. *(spoken)*
The book you are looking **for** is on the kitchen table. *(Relpronomen entfällt) (spoken)*

The problem **about which** he thinks is very difficult. *(**über das / welches**) (written)*
The problem **which / that** he thinks **about** is very difficult. *(spoken)*
The problem he thinks **about** is very difficult. *(Relpronomen entfällt) (spoken)*
*Anmerkung: **Vor that** darf **keine Präposition** stehen.*

4. Fall:

The photo **which / that** you took of Tom is wonderful. *(... das / welches ...)*
The photo you took of Tom is wonderful. *(Relativpronomen entfällt)*

The house **which / that** you see over there is my aunt's. *(... das / welches ...)*
The house you see over there is my aunt's. *(Relativpronomen entfällt)*

---

3. THAT <u>should be</u> used

   a) after: all, everything, everybody, something, somebody, someone, anything, anybody, anyone, nothing, nobody, no one, much, little, few, the only, ...

   b) after superlatives: the first, the last, the best, the most exciting ...

   c) when referring to a person *and* an animal / thing at the same time
   *(wenn sich das Relativpronomen auf eine **Person und ein Tier / Ding gleichzeitig** bezieht)*

---

ad a) **1. Fall:**

All **that** saw him were deeply moved.
Everybody **that** liked him was shocked at his behaviour.

4. Fall:

This is *all* **(that)** I can say to you.
There isn't *much* **(that)** we can do now.
Is there *something* **(that)** I can do for you?
Everything **(that)** she told you is true.
*(Hier kann **that** entfallen.)*

ad b) **1. Fall:**

The last person **that** comes must pay.
The first child **that** finds the solution will be the winner.

4. Fall:

He is **the first** man **(that)** she really likes.
This is **the best** book **(that)** I have ever read.
(*Hier kann **that** wieder **entfallen**.*)

ad c) ***The man and the dog* (that)** we met at the farm went to town.
***The girl and the cat* (that)** we saw in the garden were afraid of the dog.

4. WHICH: also refers to a sentence *(bezieht sich auch auf einen Satz)*

He told us that he had no money ⇐ **which** was not true.
We had to sleep without a blanket ⇐ **which** was terribly cold.
She was very late for school ⇐ **which** made her teacher angry.

5. WHAT = the thing / things that = that which *(das was)*

The things that / That which we saw there frightened us. =
What we saw there frightened us.

The things that / That which he heard made him sad. =
What he heard made him sad.

When father sees *the things that* you've done he'll be angry. =
When father sees **what** you've done he'll be angry.

I didn't understand *that which* he shouted. =
I didn't understand **what** he shouted.

What I don't like is people smoking in the living room.

WHO WHICH THAT WHAT

1. The woman .... we helped yesterday is Nancy's mother.
2. This is the poor little boy .... parents died in a car accident.
3. The man .... you wrote a letter will phone tomorrow.
4. The dog .... you fed last week comes for his sausage every day.
5. Who was the girl .... we met in the park?
6. Don't touch the books .... are on the table. They are father's.
7. The name of the dog .... you gave the bone is Rex.
8. The keys .... you have been looking are in your car.
9. The keys .... you have been looking .... are in your car.
10. All .... he does is clever.
11. There was no one .... was able to lift the stone.
12. This is the family .... we collected some money.
13. This is the family .... we collected some money ....
14. You should tell the police about the man .... was in your neighbour's garden.
15. The old man and his dog .... we meet in the park every day have not been there today.
16. The jeans .... belt is brown are Susan's.
17. I don't understand .... you mean.
18. The last guests .... came were Mr and Mrs Clark.
19. We had to look for her ring in the dark, ... was nearly impossible.
20. .... I really don't like is beer and gin.
21. Tell her .... she wants to know.
22. Tell her everything .... she wants to know.
23. The child .... you sent a parcel .... was very happy.
24. Last night's film was the most thrilling film .... she had ever seen.
25. Who is the man .... you saw Linda .... ?
26. Tom Hanks is one of the best actors .... Hollywood has got now.
27. Mum will go crazy if she sees .... you've done in the kitchen.
28. Unfortunately there's not much .... we can do for him.
29. I didn't remember his name, ... was very embarrassing.
30. The man .... you wanted to speak .... will come at four.
31. The driver .... the police arrested had caused a terrible accident.
32. There is only little cake .... is left in the fridge.
33. Fred was really nice to her, ... made her so happy.
34. I don't remember exactly .... he said to her.

35. Tim called Ben a liar, ... was rather insulting.
36. Either you do .... I told you or you can't go to Simon's party.
37. It rained heavily, ... made her unhappy.
38. He explained .... we should do if they needed us.
39. Who was the nice man .... you were talking .... last Friday?
40. .... she doesn't like at all is living near the airport.
41. I couldn't believe .... he told us yesterday.
42. The man .... she fell in love .... isn't the right one for her.
43. This is the most expensive hotel .... he has ever stayed.
44. This is the most expensive hotel .... he has ever stayed ....
45. Is there anything .... we can do for you?
46. Never put off till tomorrow .... you can do today.
47. The woman .... my brother married is German.
48. You ought to decide .... you want to become after school.
49. He gave her all the love .... he could give her.
50. I don't think he wanted to hear .... I said.
51. The jokes .... Roger told us were very funny.
52. Finally I've found the lamp .... I was looking .... for a long time. It's the nicest lamp .... we could find for the living room.
53. Do you understand .... he wants to tell us?
54. I was not at all interested in .... he was talking about.
55. I couldn't eat the soup, ... was too salty.
56. The sweater .... you are wearing today is trendy.
57. Mary buys her children everything .... they want.
58. You must tell him .... you really want.
59. We had a very nice weekend, ... we enjoyed very much.
60. She had to wear wet jeans, ... was most uncomfortable.
61. That's not .... I asked for.
62. The boy .... parents won the first prize is very happy now.
63. The tracksuit .... I bought for Tom wasn't very expensive.
64. Please don't tell anybody .... happened to us.
65. The dog .... bone I found in our garden is Bello.
66. The dog .... bit Mr Jones was our neighbour's dog.
67. That's exactly .... I wanted to say.
68. Father wants to do some repair work himself, ... is cheaper.
69. The glass .... he drank .... was dirty.
70. He told us about his stay in India, ... was very interesting.
71. All .... I've eaten today is an apple and a banana.
72. The house .... the Millers live is very big.
73. The house .... the Millers live .... is very big.

74. The man .... Frank was waiting .... didn't turn up.
75. The man .... Frank was waiting didn't turn up.
76. The sun was shining brightly, ... made her very happy.
77. .... I'd like now is a nice cup of tea.
78. The girl .... they laughed .... was very sad.
79. The girl .... they laughed was very sad.
80. Where is the newspaper .... I bought this morning?
81. The boy and the snake .... we saw yesterday live in apartment two.
82. The swarm of bees .... was in our garden was taken away by the fire brigade.
83. She went red in the face, ... made everybody smile.
84. That's the boy .... Nelly constantly dreams ....
85. He said that Ann would arrive at four, ... was not true.
86. Who knows .... he will do next!
87. All .... glitters is not gold.
88. She is the most charming woman .... I've ever met.
89. He was against everything .... we suggested.
90. He is the greatest boxer .... ever lived.
91. He promised to pay everything, ... was a lie.
92. The man .... name I have forgotten is Sharon's new friend.
93. The bear .... he wanted to hunt was extremely dangerous.
94. Do you know .... the sign means?
95. The beds .... we had to sleep .... were too soft.
96. He is the best teacher .... we have ever had.
97. The boy .... you said hello .... is Jimmy's brother.
98. The room .... windows open into the garden is very big.
99. Somebody .... nobody had seen before helped her change the tyre.
100. The boy .... told you this nonsense was a fool.
101. The woman .... he married is very helpful.
102. The girl .... hair is blue is Peter's younger sister.
103. The house .... you see in the picture is my parents'.
104. The hotel .... we were staying for two weeks was very clean.
105. The hotel .... we were staying .... for two weeks was very clean.
106. He is the nicest man .... I have ever met.
107. Unfortunately I didn't understand all .... the speaker announced.
108. We couldn't find any hotel .... we wanted to stay ....
109. The letter must be of somebody .... you know very well.
110. Uncle John speaks very fast, ... makes it very difficult to understand him.
111. I'm going to do my homework first, ... will take me about one hour.
112. Is that really all .... he has studied for his exam?
113. Sorry, I didn't listen to .... you said before.

114. The lake .... Tom fell was not very deep.
115. The lake .... Tom fell .... was not very deep.
116. The photo .... the guests were looking .... showed me and my brother as babies.
117. The man .... car is in front of the shop is Mr Ford, our neighbour.
118. The train .... he arrived was late.
119. Is he really the man .... we are looking ....?
120. Is he really the man .... we are looking ?
121. The girl .... went pale in the face is Nancy Carter.
122. He has got a lot of precious stamps .... he keeps in a folder.
123. The man .... you wanted to talk .... has just left.
124. The ring .... I can't find now was a present from my granny.
125. This is the woman .... purse has been stolen.
126. The music .... he prefers listening .... is jazz.
127. I'm sorry but I gave you all .... I've got. There's nothing more .... I can give you.
128. The blouse .... sleeves are long is mine.
129. That's the man .... house has burned down.
130. The boy .... is sitting next to Aunt Jane is my brother.
131. This is the girl .... mother came to see the teacher.
132. All the people .... I have asked about her don't like her.
133. The milk .... you wanted to serve for breakfast was sour.
134. I invited the woman .... I met at the concert to tea tomorrow.
135. The book .... you gave me last week is really interesting.
136. Here comes the man .... I got the bad news ....
137. Here comes the man .... I got the bad news.
138. The exams .... he must concentrate .... start in May.
139. The few coloured stones .... she found in the river made her happy.
140. We went skiing last weekend, ... was very exhausting for us.
141. All the children .... take part in the competition will win a little prize.
142. She is the only person .... has ever understood him.
143. All .... we can do now is wait.
144. Her parents always tell her .... to do.
145. I have no idea .... he means. Everything .... he tells us is so confusing.
146. I can't believe .... she told Sam.
147. She can never make up her mind, ... is really terrible.
148. The boy .... the dog was running fell down.
149. The boy .... the dog was running .... fell down.
150. The girl .... watch I've got here is in the shower.
151. These are the people .... live next door.
152. The garden .... flowers smell wonderful belongs to Mr Smith.

REFLEXIVE PRONOUNS

myself	I can do the homework **myself**.
yourself	Did you paint this picture **yourself**?
himself	Tom makes the bed **himself** in the morning.
herself	Sue can see **herself** in the mirror.
itself	The dog eats all the bone **itself**.
ourselves	We do the cooking **ourselves**.
yourselves	Did you plant the trees **yourselves**?
themselves	The vampires changed **themselves** into bats.
oneself	One should always behave **oneself**.

Study the difference:

They love **each other**.	*einander, gegenseitig*
They love **themselves**.	*sich selbst*
They hardly know **each other**.	*einander*
You hardly know **yourself**.	*dich selbst*
We looked at **each other**.	*einander, gegenseitig*
We looked at **ourselves** in the mirror.	*uns selbst*
We helped **each other**.	*einander*
We helped **ourselves** to another slice of cake.	*sich selbst bedienen*
We understood **each other**.	*einander*
I fear she doesn't understand **herself**!	*sich selbst*
We didn't see **each other**.	*einander*
We didn't see **ourselves** in the looking glass.	*uns selbst*
They didn't speak to **each other**.	*miteinander*
Old people sometimes speak to **themselves**.	*mit sich selbst*
Do they often write to **each other**?	*einander*
She wrote a letter to **herself**.	*sich selbst*

She wants to stay *by* **herself**.   *allein*
He went on holiday *by* **himself**.   *allein*
Liz lives *by* **herself**.   *allein*

Attention: We **DO NOT** use the reflexive pronoun **in English**:

He **apologized**.	*Er **entschuldigte sich**.*
They **are afraid of** the dark.	*Sie **fürchten sich** vor der Dunkelheit.*
Hurry up!	***Beeile dich**!*
Please **dress** quickly. It is late.	***Zieh dich** schnell an, bitte. Es ist spät.*
We **hid** behind the sofa.	*Wir **versteckten uns** hinter dem Sofa.*
We **looked about** us.	*Wir **sahen uns um**.*
He does not **move**.	*Er **bewegt sich** nicht.*
I'll **lie down** a bit.	*Ich werde **mich** etwas **niederlegen**.*
Sit down!	***Setz dich**! / **Setzt euch**!*
They **fell in love**.	*Sie **verliebten sich**.*
The door **opened**.	*Die Tür **öffnete sich**.*
I **remember** her well.	*Ich **erinnere mich** gut an sie.*
She still **remembers** Mark.	*Sie **erinnert sich** noch immer an M.*
We **met** in front of the park.	*Wir **trafen uns** vor dem Park.*
We **kissed**.	*Wir **küssten uns**.*

Fill in the suitable pronouns **where necessary**:

1. Call the ambulance quickly! Tom has hurt ……………… .
2. Sue never burns ……………… when she lights a candle.
3. Paul cut ……………… badly when he used his father's knife.
4. Come on, let's amuse ……………… !
5. The old lady often speaks to ……………… .
6. Linda likes to look at ……………… in the looking glass.
7. Rick and Pam write to ……………… once a month.
8. The man was depressive and killed ……………… one night.
9. Larry had to apologize ……………… .
10. The little bird did not move ……………… .
11. Little Susan can dress ……………… without her mother's help.
12. The door opened ……………… slowly.
13. Mum knitted this pullover ……………… .
14. Tell me where I should hide ……………… .
15. Phil is funny! He writes letters to ……………… .
16. I must clean my shoes ……………… .
17. Mr Rich bought a diamond ring for ……………… .

18. The Millers are going to buy .... a new car.
19. I think I'll get .... a Coke now.
20. Mr Busy did everything in his house by ....
21. Tom fell down and hurt ....
22. Enjoy .... !
23. He should look after .... better.
24. The children make all their presents for Christmas ....
25. Do you have to buy your clothes .... ?
26. He always makes a fool of ....
27. He doesn't know how to behave ....
28. Nelly only thinks about ....
29. The killer shot ....
30. I always pay for ....
31. I must lie .... down a bit, I'm tired.
32. The children give .... presents.
33. If you can't help me, I'll do it ....
34. Little Ben can climb the steps ....
35. Sheila made .... a wonderful blue dress.
36. We met .... in Park Road on Friday.
37. Sarah and Tina like .... very much.
38. You really ought to behave .... !
39. Little Liz sometimes sings to ....
40. Let me see for ....
41. The doctor tried the drug out on ....
42. Please help .... to some more coffee.
43. We sat .... down in the front row.
44. She wants to live by .... now, in a flat of her own.
45. Tim made all his furniture ....
46. Look! The dog can open the door .... !
47. Where did he hide .... ?
48. Try to be just .... !
49. We try to do as much as we can ....
50. We didn't enjoy .... very much at the funfair.
51. Our neighbours built their house ....
52. The window opened ....
53. Mum, can we help .... to some more cake?
54. We ought to hurry .... up.
55. She introduced .... to her new neighbours.
56. Tommy managed to repair his flat tyre ....
57. Don't pay for me. I'd like to pay for ....
58. Susan fell off her bike, but luckily she didn't hurt ....

PASSIVE

> **1. Formation of the passive**
>
> Form of *to be* + Past Participle
> Object becomes subject, subject becomes object

Examples:

Present Simple: Dad **does** the washing-up every day.
The washing-up **is done** by dad every day.
(*Expression of time at the end or the beginning of the sentence!*)

Present Progressive: They **are digging** up the road at the moment.
The road **is being dug** up at the moment.

Past Simple: Sally **invited** me for dinner.
I **was invited** for dinner by Sally.

Past Progressive: They **were repairing** the road during the holidays.
The road **was being repaired** during the holidays.

Present Perfect: I **haven't baked** the cake yet.
The cake **hasn't been baked** yet.

Past Perfect: They ran away after they **had broken** the window.
They ran away after the window **had been broken**.

Will-Future: They **will open** the museum on September 15th.
The museum **will be opened** on September 15th.

Going to-Future: I'**m going to** paint my room.
My room **is going to be painted**.

Conditional: They **would sell** their car.
Their car **would be sold**.

Modal Verbs:	We **can find** a solution.
A solution **can be found**.

They **could see** the flames.
The flames **could be seen**.

You **must do** your homework.
Your homework **must be done**.

He **may invite** us.
We **may be invited** by him.

They **should not allow** children to stay out after dark.
Children **should not be allowed** to stay out after dark.

They **ought to give** him a medal.
He **ought to be given** a medal.

2. Use of the passive

A) **To emphasize** (*um hervorzuheben*):
If the doer (*der Handelnde*) **is important we use the *by-object*.**

The washing-up is always done <u>by dad</u>.
The window was broken <u>by Tom</u> (*not by me!*).

B) **To give some further information:** (*für Zusatzinformationen*)

The clothes are made <u>by hand</u>.
This bird can be seen <u>only in the South of Africa</u>.

C) **If the doer (the subject) is not known or not important.**
No *by-object*.

Many school articles were stolen.
Bikes are stolen nearly daily.
Her books are sold all over the world.

D) If there are *two objects*, *two passive forms* are possible:

My husband gave *__me a wonderful ring__*.
I was given a wonderful ring by my husband.
A wonderful ring was given *to me* by my husband.
(*Der dritte Fall wird mit **to** angehängt.*)

The postman brought *__me a heavy parcel__*.
I was brought a heavy parcel.
A heavy parcel was brought **to me**.
(*Der dritte Fall wird mit **to** angehängt.*)

Verbs that may take two objects are: allow, ask, bring, give, make, offer, order, pay, promise, send, show, teach, tell, write ...

E) We do **not** write the **by-object**, if the doer is not important or if the subject is

Somebody,   **People,**
Nobody,   **They, ...**

They speak English all over the world.
English is spoken all over the world. (*No by-object!*)

Somebody helped her.
She was helped. (*No by-object!*)

F) Don't forget the prepositions!

They told me **about** the accident.
I was told **about** the accident. (*No by-object!*)

People shouted **at** the man.
The man was shouted **at**. (*No by-object!*)

Nobody slept **in** this bed last night.
This bed wasn't slept **in** last night. (*No by-object!*)

You must work **for** your success.
Your success must be worked **for**.

PUT INTO PASSIVE VOICE

1. Mary looked after her baby brother.
2. The police will catch the thief.
3. Sharon will invite us to her party next Friday.
4. They built this castle 400 years ago.
5. I'm going to write a letter.
6. Somebody broke into his house.
7. They could see the fire far away.
8. The terrible noise woke us up.
9. They destroyed the town during the war.
10. They make cheese and butter from milk.
11. You will lose your ring if you aren't careful.
12. She hasn't done her homework yet.
13. We can send her a big birthday present.
14. They may invite us.
15. The barkeeper shook the drinks.
16. We haven't found the correct answer yet.
17. Mr Smith allowed the children to play in the garden.
18. Mother won't cook lunch today.
19. They are painting the house.
20. I must iron my blouse.
21. The pupils should not eat the sandwiches during the lessons.
22. We must import bananas and oranges.
23. We could see the smoke far away.
24. Tom keeps his room very tidy.
25. He has already made some sandwiches.
26. A terrible noise in the street woke us up.
27. They were repairing the old road in the last holidays.
28. They empty the dustbins every second Thursday.
29. They haven't cut down the old oak tree yet.
30. I was angry because someone had sent the parcel to the wrong address.
31. Our neighbour's dog bit the postman.
32. They are going to sell their house in the mountains.
33. The bully punched Fred's nose.
34. He is repairing and painting the old garden fence.
35. We must make the beds before the guests come.
36. Simon gave me a book for my birthday.
37. In England pupils must wear school uniforms.
38. Father didn't prepare lunch yesterday.
39. In winter we will eat lots of fruit because of the vitamins.

40. They do not allow smoking in public places.
41. They stole his car while he was in a restaurant.
42. I was not sure if they would offer me a better job.
43. Sue won't allow you to use her car.
44. On Saturday they don't open this shop before nine.
45. You mustn't shout at children.
46. They took Mrs Brown to hospital.
47. Oliver showed us his new mountain bike.
48. They don't permit smoking at school.
49. The headmaster will give a speech at the beginning of the meeting.
50. Little Peter ate up all the sweets.
51. You may use the new computer.
52. They couldn't turn off the water.
53. They have invited her to the party.
54. You ought to learn the new words by heart.
55. The farmer is feeding the cows and the pigs.
56. They should have informed the headmaster.
57. Mr Stone is examining a pupil.
58. A new postman will deliver the letters tomorrow.
59. You can store the boxes over there.
60. You mustn't copy the homework.
61. You cannot wear those trousers. They are out of fashion.
62. You needn't help the children.
63. Paul must apply for this job.
64. They export oranges.
65. Do as they tell you.
66. We cut the grass yesterday afternoon.
67. They could solve all their problems.
68. They parked the cars in the garage.
69. Farmer John is milking the cows.
70. They should give them the right to vote.
71. Somebody took his book out of his satchel.
72. They hid the rubber boat somewhere.
73. Tomorrow they will bring the new furniture.
74. They were writing a test when the headmaster came in.
75. You may open your presents now.
76. Our neighbours will buy a flat in Vienna.
77. You may shut the window now.
78. You can't use the passive voice in this case.
79. The disease would have spread if they hadn't found the medicine.
80. The shoemaker made the shoes by hand. That's why they are so expensive.

WORDS

abroad	*im, ins Ausland*	cellar	*Keller*
accept	*annehmen*	chain	*Kette*
accident	*Unfall*	chameleon	*Chamäleon*
accurate	*genau*	chapter	*Kapitel*
admiring	*bewundernd*	cheeky	*frech*
admit	*zugeben*	choir	*Chor*
afford	*sich leisten können*	Cologne	*Köln*
aggressive	*aggressiv*	come round	*vorbeischauen*
alive (stay)	*am Leben bleiben*	competition	*Wettkampf*
all alone	*ganz alleine*	complain	*beklagen*
all of a sudden	*ganz plötzlich*	complaint	*Beschwerde*
announce	*ankündigen*	compose	*komponieren*
apologize	*sich entschuldigen*	confusing	*verwirrend*
apply for	*sich bewerben um / für*	constantly	*dauernd*
appear	*erscheinen*	cough	*Husten*
appropriate	*richtig, passend*	cover	*(Buch-)Umschlag*
Arctic Circle	*nördlicher Polarkreis*	curious	*neugierig*
artist	*Künstler*	current	*Strom*
barbecue party	*Grillparty*	customs	*Zoll*
be in	*zu Hause sein*	damage	*zerstören; Schaden*
beat	*schlagen*	Danube	*Donau*
behave	*sich benehmen*	date	*Verabredung*
behaviour	*Benehmen*	deadly	*tödlich*
believable	*glaubhaft*	deliver	*austragen (Post)*
belt	*Gürtel*	dense	*dicht*
bill	*Rechnung*	desperate	*verzweifelt*
binoculars (pl.)	*Fernglas*	diary	*Tagebuch*
blanket	*Decke*	diligent	*fleißig*
blood pressure	*Blutdruck*	dirty	*schmutzig*
book	*buchen*	disappear	*verschwinden*
boot	*Stiefel*	disease	*Krankheit*
bore	*langweilige Person*	drive somebody wild	*jemanden verrückt machen*
bossy	*herrschsüchtig*		
brake	*bremsen*	drug	*Droge*
breath	*Atem*	duly	*ordnungsgemäß*
breed	*züchten*	dustbin	*Mülltonne*
burglar	*Einbrecher*	earn	*verdienen*
burst	*zerspringen*	earthquake	*Erdbeben*
by heart	*auswendig*	electric circuit	*Stromkreis*
camping site	*Campingplatz*	embarrassing	*peinlich*
candidate	*Kandidat*	emigrate	*auswandern*
candle	*Kerze*	empty	*ausleeren, leer*
capellini	*dünne Spaghetti*	enjoy	*genießen*
carnival	*Fasching*	escape	*entkommen*
carpet	*Teppich*	even	*sogar*
case	*Fall*	exhausted	*erschöpft*
catch a cold	*sich verkühlen*	exhausting	*anstrengend*
caught (be)	*gefangen sein*	fail	*durchfallen*
cause	*verursachen*	faint	*ohnmächtig werden*
cautious	*vorsichtig*	favourite	*Lieblings-*

fear	(be)fürchten	key cutting service	Schlüsseldienst
fence	Gartenzaun	kind	freundlich
ferry	Fähre	laboratory	Labor
fine	Geldstrafe	leather	Leder
flood	überfluten	liar	Lügner
flu	Grippe	lie	Lüge
fluent	fließend	lively	lebendig
folder	Aktenmappe	looking glass	Spiegel
fond of (be)	etwas gerne tun / haben	mad	verrückt
fool	Dummkopf	madly in love	total verliebt
fool around	Blödsinn machen	married (be)	verheiratet sein
fortnight	vierzehn Tage	mass	Masse
frightened (be)	sich fürchten	mean	bedeuten, meinen
frightening	furchterregend	melt	schmelzen
front row	erste Reihe	mend	stopfen
fry	braten	mention	erwähnen
garden fence	Gartenzaun	message	Botschaft
generous	freigebig	Metaxa	griechischer Weinbrand
get rid of	loswerden	meteor	Meteor
gigantic	riesengroß	milk	melken
glitter	glänzen	mirror	Spiegel
glove	Handschuh	mischief	Unsinn
glow	glühen	mow	mähen
go with	passen zu	mud	Schlamm
goal	Tor (Fußball)	naked eye	bloßes Auge
grateful	dankbar	neighbour	Nachbar
greasy	schmierig	nos(e)y	neugierig
greedy	gierig	note	Notiz
guest	Gast	oak tree	Eiche
hail	hageln	observe	beachten
hand-me-downs	Second-Hand-Kleidung	offer	Angebot
heart (by)	auswendig	old-fashioned	altmodisch
heat	Hitze	outsider	Außenseiter
hedgehog	Igel	overnight	über Nacht
help oneself to	sich bedienen	oxygen	Sauerstoff
hoover	staubsaugen	pale	blass
hurt	verletzen	patient	geduldig
husband	Ehemann	perfume	Parfum
imagine	sich etwas vorstellen	permit	erlauben
in my place	an meiner Stelle	perpetual (ice)	ewig
incredible	unglaubhaft	pint of beer	Halbe/Glas Bier
indeed	tatsächlich	plaster	Gips
inhabitant	Einwohner	pleased	erfreut
injured	verletzt	plump	mollig
instructions	Anweisungen	powder	Puder
insulting	beleidigend	practise	üben
intense	intensiv	precious	wertvoll
interrupt	unterbrechen	prepare	zubereiten
introduce (to)	sich vorstellen bei	pressure	Druck
invention	Erfindung	print	drucken
invitation	Einladung	prism	Prisma
jealous	eifersüchtig	private industry	Privatindustrie
jog	joggen		
journey	Reise		

probable	wahrscheinlich	spectator	Zuschauer
probably	wahrscheinlich	speech	Rede
properly	gewissenhaft	spider	Spinne
protection	Schutz	spinach	Spinat
pump out	auspumpen	spray can	Spraydose
punch	schlagen	spread	ausbreiten
purse	Geldtasche	spring	Frühling
put off	aufschieben	sprinter	Läufer
put out	löschen	stay alive	am Leben bleiben
rarely	selten	store	lagern
realistic	realistisch	succeed	Erfolg haben
receive	empfangen	successful	erfolgreich
recently	neulich, in letzter Zeit	suggest	vorschlagen
recipe	Rezept	suntan	Sonnenbräune
recite	aufsagen	surprised	überrascht
recognise (BE)	erkennen	suspect	Verdächtiger
recognize (AE)	erkennen	swarm	Schwarm
relaxed	entspannt	swear	schwören
relaxing	erholsam	tail	Schwanz
remark	bemerken	take off (plane)	starten
restore	restaurieren	take part in	teilnehmen an
rid (get rid of)	loswerden	talk back	zurückschnabeln
ridiculous	lächerlich	tap	Wasserhahn
rotten	verdorben	tease	necken
rubber boat	Schlauchboot	though	obwohl
rule	Regel	tracksuit	Jogginganzug
rum	Rum	traffic signs	Verkehrszeichen
sail (go for a)	segeln gehen	train	trainieren
saucer	Untertasse	trendy	modern, in
scared (be)	sich fürchten	trouble	Schwierigkeit
scientist	Wissenschaftler	true	wahr
score a goal	Tor schießen	trumpet	Trompete
scratch	kratzen	truth	Wahrheit
seat	Sitz, Platz	tyre	Reifen (beim Rad/Auto)
seem true	wahr scheinen	turn sour	sauer werden
seldom	selten	twins	Zwillinge
selfish	egoistisch	unbelievable	unglaublich
serious	ernsthaft	uncomfortable	ungemütlich
set (sun)	untergehen	unfortunately	unglücklicherweise
several	einige	velvet	Samt
severe	ernstlich; streng	Venice	Venedig
shell	Muschel	vote	wählen
shoot a film	drehen	wag	wedeln
shot (be)	erschossen	walk sb. home	jemanden heimbringen
sights	Sehenswürdigkeiten	war	Krieg
skid	ausrutschen	waste	verschwenden
sleeve	Ärmel	wife	Ehefrau
slim	schlank; abnehmen	windscreen	Windschutzscheibe
slippery	rutschig	worry	sich Sorgen machen
smother (flame)	ersticken (Flamme)	wounded	verwundet
so far	bisher, bis jetzt	yuk	pfui
soccer	Fußball		
solution	Lösung		

KEY

pages 4, 5

1. do (☺ I, p 50)
2. went, bought (☺ I, p 76/77)
3. have already finished (☺ II, p 68)
4. was working, was cooking (☺ II, p 79) / is working, is cooking
5. sleeps (☺ I, p 50)
6. has just written (☺ II, p 68)
7. has never had (☺ II, p 68)
8. was sleeping (☺ II, p 79)
9. are, is going to hail (☺ II, p 47)
10. is going to come (☺ II, p 47, *persönlicher Plan*)
11. have not phoned (☺ II, p 68)
12. were (☺ I, p 76/77)
13. have not seen (☺ II, p 68)
14. are going (☺ III, p 15), (☺ I, p 82 Merke)
15. does (☺ I, p 50)
16. is climbing (☺ I, p 51/52)
17. have already done (☺ II, p 68)
18. got (☺ I, p 76/77)
19. is going to shout (☺ II, p 47)
20. leaves (☺ I, p 50)
21. was reading, entered, asked, wanted (☺ II, p 79/3)
    Anmerkung: **if** heißt hier **ob**, daher darf **some**thing stehen! Vergleiche: (☺ II, p 19/3)
22. come (☺ I, p 50)
23. have not seen (☺ II, p 68)
24. has studied (☺ II, p 68, *wir befinden uns am Ende der Woche*) /
    is going to study (☺ II, p 47, *wir befinden uns am Anfang der Woche, persönlicher Plan*) /
    is studying (☺ I, p 51, *wir befinden uns mitten in der Woche*)
25. am writing (☺ I, p 51/52)
26. was learning, came (☺ II, p 79/3)
27. was, caught (☺ I, p 76/77)
28. are looking forward to (☺ I, p 51/52)
29. stole, was (☺ I, p 76/77)
30. will be (☺ II, p 45/ 46)
31. meets, asks, are (☺ I, p 50) /
    met, asked, were (☺ I, p 76/77, *Mrs Franklin ist gestorben, daher Past tense*)
32. have you been, have tried (☺ II, p 68)
33. do you spend (☺ I, p 50)
34. did you spend (☺ I, p 76/77), are you going to spend (☺ II, p 47)
35. began, ste**pp**ed (☺ I, p 76/77)
36. are you going to stay (☺ II, p 47)
37. will be (☺ II, p 45/46)
38. will never talk (☺ II, p 45/46)
39. were di**gg**ing, found (☺ II, p 79/3)
40. will have (☺ II, p 45/46) / had
41. is, have not yet arrived (☺ II, p 68)
42. has had (☺ II, p 68)
43. were eating, attacked (☺ II, p 79/3)
44. broke, filled (☺ I, p 76/77, *zwei kurze, aufeinanderfolgende Handlungen*)
45. have not understood (☺ II, p 68) /
    don't understand (☺ I, p 52, *understand: no progressive form*)
46. have never had (☺ II, p 68)
47. will pick / 'll pick you up (☺ II, p 45/C)
48. Have you already heard (☺ II, p 68), broke, fell (☺ I, p 76/77, *zwei kurze, aufeinanderfolgende Handlungen*), is
49. was riding, jumped, bit (☺ II, p 79/3)
50. is packing, is writing (☺ I, p 51/52) / was packing, was writing (☺ II, p 79/2)
51. is frying (☺ I, p 51/52) / has fried (☺ II, p 68)
52. is he doing, is ge**tt**ing, is taking, is hurrying (☺ I, p 51/52)

page 6

1. It took father two hours to iron the shirts.
2. It will take me an / one hour to write the essay.
3. It took us half a day to go to the sea.
4. It will take father two months to repair the garden fence.
5. It usually takes him more than an / one hour to drink / have his tea.
6. It took the children some hours to build the sandcastle.
7. It doesn't take us more than fifteen minutes to put up the tent.
8. It took Betty two days to sew / make her dress.
9. It took the fire brigade three hours to put out the fire.
10. It took us five hours to climb the mountain.
11. It will take him years to get over her death.
12. It normally takes me ten minutes to go to school.
13. It will take granny two hours to plant the flowers.
14. It took Tom an / one hour to pack the suitcase.

page 8

1. will catch (Regel 2, *bestimmte, einmalige Situation*)
2. will be able to (☺ II, p 6) / can (2)
3. will get (2)
4. send (1, *Bitte, Aufforderung*)
5. always gets (1, *das ist immer so, Tatsache*)
6. won't get (2, *bestimmte, einmalige Situation*)
7. don't go (1, *Bitte, Aufforderung*)
8. will be (2, *bestimmte, einmalige Situation*)
9. give (1, *Bitte, Aufforderung*)
10. will stay (2, *bestimmte, einmalige Situation*)
11. bursts (1, *das ist immer so, allgemeingültige Tatsache*)
12. may / will be allowed to (2, *bestimmte, einmalige Situation*) (☺ II, p / 6)
13. doesn't speak (1, *das ist immer so, allgemeingültige Tatsache*)
14. will get (2, *bestimmte, einmalige Situation*)
15. won't go (2, *bestimmte, einmalige Situation*)
16. will look (2, *bestimmte, einmalige Situation*)
17. will be (2, *bestimmte, einmalige Situation*)
18. is (1, *das ist immer so, Tatsache*)
19. turns (1, *das ist immer so, Tatsache*)
20. don't forget (1, *Bitte, Aufforderung*)

21. will be (2, *bestimmte, einmalige Situation*)
22. hand (1, *Bitte, Aufforderung*)
23. will make (2, *bestimmte, einmalige Situation*)
24. won't get (2, *bestimmte, einmalige Situation*)
25. are (1, *das ist immer so, Tatsache*)
26. will take (2, *bestimmte, einmalige Situation*)
27. tells (1, *das ist immer so, Tatsache*)
28. won't help (2, *bestimmte, einmalige Situation*)
29. is (1, *das ist so, Tatsache*)

page 10

1. would be / 'd be
2. would be / 'd be
3. asked
4. knew
5. would be
6. told
7. knew
8. could / were able to
9. could / would be able to
10. helped
11. could / would be able to
12. would arrest
13. would look
14. could / would be able to
15. could / would be able to
16. drank
17. waited
18. would be
19. were / was (*spoken English*)
20. found
21. wanted
22. weren't / wasn't (*spoken English*)
23. would succeed
24. could / would be able to
25. were / was (*spoken English*)
26. would have
27. would not believe / wouldn't believe
28. would not believe / wouldn't believe
    Anmerkung: Sätze 27, 28 bedeuten dasselbe!
29. would have to walk (*must = have to* ☺ II p 7)

pages 11, 12, 13

1. could / were able to (☺ III p 9)
2. can / will be able to (☺ III p 7/2, *best.Situation*)
3. will have (☺ III p 7/2, *bestimmte Situation*)
4. will fall (☺ III p 7/2, *bestimmte Situation*)
5. will not help (☺ III p 7/2, *bestimmte Situation*)
6. needs (☺ III p 7/2, *bestimmte Situation*)
7. will come (☺ III p 7/2, *bestimmte Situation*)
8. would not do (☺ III p 9)
9. worked (☺ III p 9)
10. do not stop / don't stop (☺ III p 7/2, *best. Situation*)
11. were / was (*spoken English*) (☺ III p 9)
12. cannot / won't be able to (☺ III p 7/2, *best. Sit.*)
13. would answer (☺ III p 9)
14. asked (☺ III p 9)
15. will look (☺ III p 7/2, *bestimmte Situation*)
16. melts (☺ III p 7/1, *Tatsache, Naturgesetz*)
17. would look (☺ III p 9)
18. will look (☺ III p 7/2, *bestimmte Situation*)
19. did not want / didn't want (☺ III p 9)
20. can / will be able to (☺ III p 7/2, *best. Situation*)
21. may / will be allowed to (☺ III p 7/2, *best. Sit.*)
22. weren't / wasn't (*spoken English*) (☺ III p 9)
23. would have (☺ III p 9)
24. swims (☺ III p 7/1, *Tatsache, Naturgesetz*)
25. give (☺ III p 7/2, *bestimmte Situation*)
26. didn't eat / did not eat (☺ III p 9)
27. will fall (☺ III p 7/2, *bestimmte Situation*)
28. could / would be able to (☺ III p 9)
29. would pass (☺ III p 9)
30. would give (☺ III p 9)
31. were / was (*spoken English*) (☺ III p 9)
32. would be (☺ III p 9)
33. must / will have to (☺ III p 7/2, *best. Situation*)
34. could / would be able to (☺ III p 9)
35. drank (☺ III p 9)
36. would have to (☺ III p 9, ☺ II p 7: *must = have to*)
37. will make (☺ III p 7/2, *bestimmte Situation*)
38. would earn (☺ III p 9)
39. asks (☺ III p 7/2, *bestimmte Situation*)
40. will break (☺ III p 7/2, *bestimmte Situation*)
41. would buy (☺ III p 9)
42. would be (☺ III p 9)
43. must / will have to (☺ III p 7/2, *best. Situation*)
44. am (☺ III p 7/2, *bestimmte Situation*)
45. will stay (☺ III p 7/2, *bestimmte Situation*)
46. will thank (☺ III p 7/2, *bestimmte Situation*)
47. is (☺ III p 7/2, *bestimmte Situation*)
48. do not go / don't go (☺ III p 7/2, *best. Situation*)
49. talks (☺ III p 7/1, *allgemeingültige Aussage, das ist immer so mit Sam*)
50. would you do (☺ III p 9)
51. tell (☺ III p 7/1, *Bitte, Aufforderung*)
52. do not do / don't do (☺ III p 7/2, *best. Situation*)
53. will be (☺ III p 7/2, *bestimmte Situation*)
54. would believe (☺ III p 9)
55. damage (☺ III p 7/1, *allgemeingültige Aussage, Tatsache*)
56. weren't / wasn't (*spoken English*) (☺ III p 9)
57. will see (☺ III p 7/2, *bestimmte Situation*)
58. would be / 'd be (☺ III p 9)
59. will get (☺ III p 7/2, *bestimmte Situation*) / gets (☺ III p 7/1, *allgemeingültige Aussage, das ist immer so mit ihrem Vater*)
60. will get (☺ III p 7/2, *bestimmte Situation*)
61. will not pass / won't pass (☺ III p 7/2, *best.Sit.*)
62. will not fly / won't fly (☺ III p 7/2, *bestimmte Situation*)
63. hear (☺ III p 7/2, *bestimmte Situation*)
64. would call (☺ III p 9)
65. could / would be able to (☺ III p 9)
66. will go (☺ III p 7/2, *bestimmte Situation*)
67. comes (☺ III p 7/1, *Bitte, Aufforderung*)
68. will probably get (☺ III p 7/2, *bestimmte Situation*)
69. weren't / wasn't (*spoken English*) (☺ III p 9)
70. will take (☺ III p 7/2, *bestimmte Situation*)
71. would have to (☺ III p 9, ☺ II p 7: *must = have to*)
72. would not swim / wouldn't swim (☺ III p 9)
73. were / was (*spoken English*) (☺ III p 9)
74. drank (☺ III p 9), would rise (☺ III p 9)
75. stops (☺ III p 7/2, *bestimmte Situation*)
76. will arrive (☺ III p 7/2, *bestimmte Situation*)
77. would have (☺ III p 9)
78. could / would be able to (☺ III p 9)
79. goes (☺ III p 7/2, *bestimmte Situation*)
80. is not / isn't (☺ III p 7/1, *allgemeingültige Aussage, Tatsache*)

81. turns (☺ III p 7/1, *allgemeingültige Aussage, Tatsache, Naturgesetz*)
82. will be (☺ III p 7/2, *bestimmte Situation*)
83. inform (☺ III p 7/1, *Bitte, Aufforderung*)
84. would have to (☺ III p 9, ☺ II p 7: *must = have to*)
85. lived (☺ III p 9)
86. must / have to (☺ III p 7/1, *allgemeingültige Aussage, Tatsache*)
87. called (☺ III p 9)
88. do not mind / don't mind (☺ III p 7/2, *best. Situat.*)
89. would have to (☺ III p 9, ☺ II p 7: *must = have to*)
90. came (☺ III p 9)
91. would accept (☺ III p 9)
92. would be (☺ III p 9)
93. worried (☺ III p 9)
94. may (☺ III p 7/2)
95. will lose (☺ III p 7/2)

page 14

1. When (*Es ist sicher, dass ich dort bin.*)
2. If (*Es ist unsicher, ob überhaupt ein Brief da ist.*)
3. If (*Es ist unsicher, ob er / sie etwas aus der Stadt braucht.*)
4. If (*Es ist unsicher, ob er/sie mir nicht helfen kann.*)
5. If (*Es ist unsicher, ob morgen Schnee ist.*)
6. When (*Es ist sicher, dass ich das Video ansehe.*)
7. when (*immer wieder*)
8. If (*Wir würden ihr helfen, falls ...*)
9. if (*Es ist unsicher, wie das Wetter morgen ist.*)
10. If (*Es ist unsicher, ob er / sie zu Sally fährt.*) / When (*Es ist sicher, dass er / sie zu Sally fährt.*)
11. When (*Es ist sicher, dass sie von der Schule heimkommt, und sie duscht jedes Mal.*)
12. If (*Es ist unsicher, ob noch Karten vorhanden sind.*)
13. If (*Es ist unsicher, ob wir uns morgen treffen.*)
14. if (*Es ist unsicher, ob es jemandem etwas ausmacht.*)
15. When (*Es ist sicher, dass er zur Arbeit geht, und er nimmt immer wieder seinen Schirm mit.*)
16. If (*Bedingung: Falls du so viel trinkst, wirst du morgen krank sein.*)
17. If (*Bedingung: falls du nicht zurück bist, wird Mutter nervös sein.*)

pages 17, 18

Anmerkung:
Die Zukunft kann auf verschiedene Weise ausgedrückt werden. Hier einige **Vorschläge** *zu den häufigsten Anwendungsfällen.*
Je nach Absicht des Sprechers oder je nach Situation *passt eine Form. Es gibt daher meist* **mehrere Lösungsmöglichkeiten.**

1. will you be doing (☺ III p 16/3, *bestimmter zukünftiger Zeitpunkt*)
2. is going to meet (☺ II p 47 A/C) / is meeting (☺ III p 15/1, *Ersatz für going to für persönlichen, zukünftigen Plan*)
3. will buy (☺ III p 7/2)
4. will recognise (☺ II p 45/46, *think*)
5. are going to have (☺ II p 47 A/C) / are having (☺ III p 15/1, *Ersatz für going to für persönlichen, zukünftigen Plan*)
6. will mend (☺ II p 45/46 C, *spontane Entscheidung*)
7. arrives; leaves (☺ III p 16/2, *Subjekt keine Person, Fahrplan*); won't have (☺ II p 45/46 A, *neutrale Zukunft, Befürchtung*) / are not going to have (☺ II p 47, *Sprecher ist sich ganz sicher*)
8. will be taking (☺ III p 16/3, *best. zukünft. Zeitpunkt*)
9. leaves (☺ III p 16/2, *Subjekt keine Pers., Fahrplan*)
10. will you be having (☺ III p 16/3, *best. zuk. Zeitpkt*) / are you going to have (☺ II p 47 A/C, *persönl. Plan*)
11. Will there be (☺ II p 45/46 B, *neutrale Zukunft für formelle Termine*)
12. will possibly send (☺ II p 45/46 A, *possibly*)
13. is travelling (☺ III p 15/1, *Subjekt ist Person, Verb der Bewegung*) / is going to travel (☺ II p 47 A/C, *persönl. Plan*)
14. Will you have (☺ II p 45/46 C)
15. open (☺ II p 88, *as soon as + Present*)
16. does the plane arrive (☺ III p 16/2, *Subjekt ist keine Person, Fahrplan*) / will ... arrive (*Neutrales Futur*)
17. is John going to do (☺ II p 47 A/C, *persönl. Plan*)
18. are going to get (☺ II p 47 A/C, *persönl. Plan*) / are getting (☺ III p 15/1)
19. Will you be passing (☺ III p 16/3, *bestimmter zukünftiger Zeitraum*) / are you going to pass (☺ II p 47 A/C), take (☺ II p 88, *when*)
20. will be working (☺ III p 16/3, *best. zuk. Zeitpunkt*)
21. starts (☺ III p 16/2, *Subjekt ist keine Person, Vorstellungsbeginn*)
22. is leaving (☺ III p 15/1, *Subjekt ist Person, Verb der Bewegung*) / is going to leave (☺ II p 47 A/C)
23. arrives (☺ III p 16/2, *Subjekt ist keine Person, Fahrplan*)
24. will help (☺ II p 45/46 C, *wait a moment: Entscheidung erfolgt während des Sprechens*)
25. will come; will be (☺ II p 45/46 B, *formelle Ankündigung*)
26. will be lying (☺ III p 16/3, *best. zukünft. Zeitpunkt*)
27. will have / 'll have (☺ II p 45/46 C, *Entscheidung erfolgt während des Sprechens*)
28. does the ship go (☺ III p 16/2, *Subjekt ist keine Person, Fahrplan*)
29. is, will have (*Conditional I,* ☺ III p 7/2)
30. will iron (☺ II p 45/46 C, *Entscheidung erfolgt während des Sprechens*)
31. are you going to do (☺ II p 47 A/C, *persönl. Plan*) / are you doing (☺ III p 15/1)
32. will be (☺ II p 45/46 E, *Bitte, Aufforderung*)
33. will be watching (☺ III p 16/3, *best. zuk. Zeitpunkt*)
34. is leaving (☺ III p 15/1, *Subjekt ist Person, Verb der Bewegung*)
35. is going to be (☺ II p 47 D, *sicher vorhersagbare Zukunft*) / will be (☺ II p 45/46 A, *Erwartung, Befürchtung*)
36. am going to listen (☺ II p 47 A/C) / am listening (☺ III p 15/1)
37. will be (☺ II p 45/46 B, *formelle Ankündigung*)
38. will like (☺ II p 45/46, *think*)
39. will be, 'll be (☺ II p 45/46 A, *Vermutung, Erwartung*)

40. will be practising (☺ III p 16/3, *best. zuk. Zeitraum*)
41. am going (☺ III p 15/1, *Verb der Bewegung*)
42. will take, 'll take (☺ II p 45/46 C, *Entscheidung erfolgt während des Sprechens*)
43. does the last bus go (☺ III p 16/2, *Subjekt ist keine Person, Fahrplan*)
44. will buy (*Conditional I*, ☺ III p7/2)
45. will rain (☺ II p 45/46, *think*)
46. am arriving (☺ III p 15/1, *Verb der Bewegung*)
47. will be having (☺ III p 16/3, *best. zuk. Zeitpunkt*)
48. will be sleeping (☺ III p 16/3, *best. zuk. Zeitpunkt*)
49. is going to go (☺ II p 47 A/C, *persönl. Plan*) / is going (☺ III p 15/1, *Verb der Bewegung*)
50. is going to faint (☺ II p 47 D, *sicher vorhersagbare Zukunft*) / will faint (☺ II p 45/46 A, *Erwartung, Befürchtung*)
51. will like (☺ II p 45/46, *hope*)
52. does the soccer match start (☺ III p 16/2, *Subjekt ist keine Person, Veranstaltungsbeginn*)
53. is dad staying away (☺ III p 15/1) / is dad going to stay away (☺ II p 47 A/C, *pers. Plan*)
54. arrives (☺ III p 16/2, *Subj. ist keine Pers., Fahrpl.*)
55. will be having (☺ III p 16/3, *best. zuk. Zeitpunkt*)
56. goes (☺ III p 16/2, *Subj. ist keine Pers., Fahrplan*)
57. will talk (☺ II p 45/46 B, *formeller Termin*)

page 19

1. any (☺ II p19 rule 1)
2. Somebody / Someone (☺ II p18 rule 1)
3. Any (☺ II p19 rule 4)
4. Any (☺ II p19 rule 4)
5. Somebody / Someone (☺ II p18 rule 1)
6. something (☺ II p18 rule 2)
7. some (☺ II p18 rule 1)
8. anybody / anyone (☺ II p19 rule 3)
9. any (☺ II p19 rule 1), some (☺ II p18 rule 1)
10. Someone / Somebody (☺ II p18 rule 1)
11. any (☺ II p19 rule 4)
12. somebody / someone / something (☺ IIp18 rule 2), anybody / anyone / anything (☺ II p19 rule 2)
13. Somewhere (☺ II p18 rule 1)
14. somehow (☺ II p18 rule 1)
15. something / some (☺ II p18 rule 2), some (☺ II p18 rule1), any (☺ II p19 rule 3)
16. anything (☺ II p19 rule 1, *hardly = kaum, Negation*)
17. any (☺ II p19 rule 3)
18. anything / anybody / anyone (☺ II p19 rule 1)
19. somewhere (☺ II p18 rule 1)
20. anything (☺ II p19 rule 4)
21. somehow (☺ II p18 rule 1)
22. any (☺ II p19 rule 1)
23. any (☺ II p19 rule 3)
24. Some (☺ II p18 rule 2) / Any (☺ II p19 rule 2), any (☺ II p19 rule 4)
25. any (☺ II p19 rule 1)
26. something (☺ II p18 rule 1), Any (☺ II p19 rule 4)
27. somehow (☺ II p18 rule 1)
28. any (☺ II p19 rule 4)
29. something (☺ II p18 rule 2) / something (☺ II p18 rule 1)
30. something / somebody / someone (☺ II p18 rule1)
31. something / somebody / someone (☺ II p18 rule1)
32. Any (☺ II p19 rule 4)

pages 22, 23, 24

*Bei den Lösungssätzen gibt es oft **mehrere** Möglichkeiten, je nachdem **was man ausdrücken will**.*

1. oughtn't to (☺ II p 12)
2. won't be able to / will be unable to (☺ II p 6), will have to (☺ II p 7)
3. needn't / don't have to / don't need to / haven't got to (☺ II p 7), was allowed to (☺ II p 6)
4. May, may (☺ II p 6, ☺ III p 21) *sehr höflich*
5. had to (☺ II p 7), couldn't / wasn't able to / was unable to (☺ II p 6)
6. should (☺ II p 12) *höflicher Vorschlag* / shall (☺ III p 20) *Aufforderung, Befehl*
7. ought to (☺ II p 12), may / might (☺ III p 21) *Befürchtung, Vermutung*
8. shall (☺ III p 20) *Aufforderung, Befehl*
9. *Present*: mustn't (☺ II p 7)
   Past: were not allowed to (☺ II p 7)
   Future: won't be allowed to (☺ II p 7)
10. should (☺ II p 12) *höflicher Vorschlag* / shall (☺ III p 20) *Aufforderung, Befehl*
11. ought to (☺ II p 12)
12. may / might (☺ III p 21) *Möglichkeit, Befürchtung, Vermutung*
13. may / might (☺ III p 21) *Möglichkeit, Vermutung*
14. can / could (☺ III p 20) / may / might (☺ III p 21) *Möglichkeit, Vermutung*
15. may / might (☺ III p 21) / could (☺ III p 20) *Befürchtung, Vermutung, Möglichkeit*
16. ought to (☺ II p 12)
17. *Past*: couldn't / wasn't able to / was unable to (☺ II p 6), had to (☺ II p 7)
    Future: won't be able to / will be unable to (☺ II p 6), will have to (☺ II p 7)
18. *Present*: needn't / don't have to / don't need to / haven't got to (☺ II p 7)
    Future: won't have to / won't need to (☺ II p 7)
19. oughtn't to (☺ II p 12)
20. shall (☺ III p 20) *Aufforderung, Befehl* / should (☺ II p 12) *höflicher Vorschlag*
21. couldn't / wasn't able to / was unable to (☺ II p 6), had to (☺ II p 7)
22. ought to (☺ II p 12)
23. has had to (☺ II p 68, 89) / will have to (☺ II p 7)
24. *Present*: needn't / doesn't have to / doesn't need to / hasn't got to (☺ II p 7)
    Past: didn't have to / didn't need to (☺ II p 7)
    Future: won't have to / won't need to (☺ II p 7)
25. have not been able to / have been unable to (☺ II p 68, 89)
26. has been allowed to (☺ II p 68, 89)
27. may / might (☺ III p 21) *Möglichkeit, Befürchtung, Vermutung*

28. could / was able to (☺ II p 6)
29. ought to (☺ II p 12)
30. has not been able to / has been unable to
    (☺ II p 68, 89)
31. didn't have to / didn't need to (☺ II p 7)
32. may / might (☺ III p 21) *Möglichkeit, Befürchtung, Vermutung*
33. has not been allowed to (☺ II p 68, 89)
34. won't be allowed to (☺ II p 6),
    may / might (☺ III p 21) *Möglichkeit, Befürchtung, Vermutung*
35. shall not (☺ III p 21) *Aufforderung, Befehl* /
    should not (☺ II p 12) *höflicher Vorschlag*
36. *Present*: needn't / don't have to / don't need to / haven't got to (☺ II p 7)
    Future: won't have to / won't need to (☺ II p 7)
37. couldn't / weren't able to / were unable to (☺ II p6)
38. can (☺ III p 20) *Angebot* /
    could (☺ III p 20) *höfliches Angebot*,
    Present: needn't / don't have to / don't need to / haven't got to (☺ II p 7)
    Future: won't have to / won't need to (☺ II p 7)
39. may not / mightn't (☺ III p 21) *Möglichkeit, Befürchtung, Vermutung*
40. shall (☺ III p 20) *Aufforderung, Befehl* /
    should (☺ II p 12) *höflicher Vorschlag*
41. won't have to / won't need to (☺ II p 7)
42. wasn't allowed to (☺ II p 7)
43. Can (☺ III p 20) *Bitte bei Familienmitgliedern* /
    Could (☺ III p 20) *höfliche Bitte*
44. needn't / don't have to / don't need to / haven't got to (☺ II p 7), will be able to (☺ II p 6)
45. couldn't / wasn't able to (☺ II p 6)
46. may / might (☺ III p 21) *Möglichkeit, Befürchtung, Vermutung* /
    can / could (☺ III p 20) *Möglichkeit*
47. shall not (☺ III p 21) *Aufforderung, Befehl* /
    should not (☺ II p 12) *höflicher Vorschlag*
48. may not / mightn't (☺ III p 21) *Befürchtung, Vermutung*
49. shall (☺ III p 20) *Vorschlag* /
    should (☺ II p 12) *höflicher Vorschlag*
50. won't be allowed to (☺ II p 7) /
    has not been allowed to (☺ II p 68, 89)
51. shall not (☺ III p 21) *Aufforderung, Befehl* /
    should not (☺ II p 12) *höflicher Vorschlag*
52. shall not (☺ III p 21) *Aufforderung, Befehl* /
    should not (☺ II p 12) *höflicher Vorschlag*
53. *Present*: must not / aren't allowed to (☺ II p 7)
    Past: weren't allowed to (☺ II p 7)
    Future: won't be allowed to (☺ II p 7)
54. *Present*: must not / isn't allowed to (☺ II p 7)
    Future: won't be allowed to (☺ II p 7)
55. ought to (☺ II p 12)
56. won't have to / won't need to (☺ II p 7)
57. shall not (☺ III p 21) *Aufforderung, Befehl* /
    should not (☺ II p 12) *höflicher Vorschlag*
58. ought to (☺ II p 12)
59. have not been able to / have been unable to
    (☺ II p 68, 89)
    Future: won't be able to / will be unable to (☺II p6)
60. won't be allowed to (☺ II p 6)
61. *Present*: needn't / don't have to / don't need to / haven't got to (☺ II p 7)
    Future: won't have to / won't need to (☺ II p 7)
62. can / could (☺ III p 20) *Möglichkeit* /
    may / might (☺ III p 21) *Möglichkeit, Vermutung, Befürchtung*
63. must (☺ II p 7)
64. may / might (☺ III p 21) *Möglichkeit, Vermutung, Befürchtung* /
    could (☺ III p 20) *Möglichkeit*
65. could (☺ III p 20) *Möglichkeit* /
    may / might (☺ III p 21) *Vermutung, Möglichkeit*
66. had to (☺ II p 7)
67. Shall (☺ III p 20) *Vorschlag* /
    Should (☺ II p 12) *höflicher Vorschlag*
68. have not been able to /
    have been unable to (☺ II p 68, 89)
69. ought to (☺ II p 12)
70. has not had to (☺ II p 68, 89)
71. will be able to (☺ II p 6) / can (☺ III p 20)
72. won't be allowed to (☺ II p 6)

pages 28, 29, 30, 31, 32

*Die Lösungsvorschläge richten sich jeweils danach, was der Sprecher **ausdrücken will**, was er **besonders betonen** möchte. Mehrere Lösungen sind bisweilen möglich.*

1. has gone (☺ III p25/1)
2. Have you *ever* been (☺ II p68, ☺ III p25/1)
3. has *just* drunk (☺ II p68, ☺ III p25/1, *Resultat: he feels sick ist wichtig*)
4. has not spoken (☺ III p25/1, *Resultat: difficulties in France wichtig*)
5. has tried (☺ II p68, ☺ III p25/1, *Handlung = Versuch beendet, weil Chinesisch für ihn zu schwierig ist*) / has been trying (☺ III p25/2: *er versucht es noch immer*)
6. has been l**y**ing (☺ III p25/2, *Handlung dauert weiter an, da John noch immer krank ist*)
7. has been staying (☺ III p25/2, *er ist noch immer dort*)
8. have known (☺ III p27, *Attention: know*)
9. have you been doing, have been working
   (☺ III p25/2, *Dauer ist wichtig*)
10. have been eating (☺ III p25/2, *Dauer ist wichtig, sie essen noch immer*)
11. have been jogging (☺ III p25/2, *Dauer und Hdlg. selbst sind wichtig*) / have jogged (☺ III p25/1, *Resultat: exhausted ist wichtig*)
12. have been trying (☺ III p25/2, *Handlung dauert noch an, sie suchen den Weg noch immer*),
    have lost (☺ III p25/1, *einmalige, beendete Handlung des Wegverlierens*)
13. have you been going (☺ III p25/2, *Handlung = Schulbesuch dauert noch an*)
14. have you been living (☺ III p25/2, *Handlung dauert noch an, er/sie lebt noch immer dort*)
15. have been shouting (☺ III p25/2, *Handlung dauert noch an, sie werden noch weiterrufen müssen, da sie noch niemand gehört hat*)
    has found (☺ II p68)
16. Have you written (☺ II p68, ☺ III p25/1, *Resultat ist wichtig: Yes, of course, Handlung beendet*)

17. have *already* tidied (☺ II p68, ☺ III p25/1, *Resultat ist wichtig*)
18. have been looking (☺ III p25/2, *Handlung dauert noch an, sie werden noch weitersuchen müssen, da sie sie noch nicht gefunden haben*), have been unable to / haven't been able to (☺ II p89)
19. have lived (☺ II p68, ☺ III p25/1, *Handlung beendet, wir werden umziehen*)
20. have you been looking (☺ III p25/2, *Handlung dauert noch an, er/sie sucht noch weiter*)
21. has painted (☺ II p68, ☺ III p25/1, *Handlung beendet, Resultat: die Wände sind wieder weiß*)
22. has been painting (☺ III p25/2, *Handlung ist wichtig und noch nicht abgeschlossen*) / has painted (☺ II p68, ☺ III p25/1, *Handlung beendet, Resultat: seine Kleidung ist voller Farbe*)
23. has repaired (☺ II p68, ☺ III p25/1, *Handlung beendet, Resultat: seine Hose ist fettig*) / has been repairing (☺ III p25/2, *Handlung ist wichtig und noch nicht abgeschlossen*)
24. have been smoking (☺ III p25/2, *Handlung ist wichtig und noch nicht abgeschlossen, er raucht noch immer*)
25. has repaired (☺ II p68, ☺ III p25/1, *Handlung beendet, Resultat: das Auto geht wieder*)
26. has used (☺ II p68, ☺ III p25/1, *Handlung beendet, Resultat: die Parfumflasche ist leer*)
27. has been writing (☺ III p25/2, *Dauer der Handlung ist wichtig und Hdlg. ist noch nicht abgeschlossen*)
28. has written (☺ II p68, ☺ III p25/1, *Handlung beendet*, ☺ III p26 / *Attention: Resultat:* **drei** *Briefe sind fertig*)
29. have you been reading (☺ III p25/2, *Handlung = Lesen ist noch nicht abgeschlossen: ist aus der Antwort: for two weeks now ersichtlich*)
30. has played (☺ II p68, ☺ III p25/1, **three** *times, wiederholte Handlung*)
31. has written (☺ II p68, ☺ III p26, *Attention:* **five** *postcards*)
32. have you read, have only read (☺ II p68, ☺ III p26, *Attention:* **sixty** *pages*)
33. has been (☺ III p27, *Attention: be*)
34. has bought (☺ II p68, ☺ III p26, *Attention:* **three** *bikes*)
35. have lost (☺ II p68, ☺ III p25/1, *einmalige Handlung des Verlierens*)
36. have you been working (☺ III p25/2, *Handlung ist besonders wichtig*) / have you worked (☺ II p68, ☺ III p25/1, *Resultat: you look tired ist besonders wichtig*)
37. has broken (☺ II p68, ☺ III p25/1, *Resultat ist wichtig: There's glass on the floor*)
38. have been reading (☺ III p25/2, *Handlung = Lesen ist noch nicht abgeschlossen*), have *not* finished (☺ II p68)
39. have been cleaning (☺ III p25/2, *Handlung = Putzen ist noch nicht abgeschlossen*), have cleaned (☺ II p68, ☺ III p26, *Attention: I have cleaned* **six**)
40. have you been cooking (☺ III p25/2, *Handlung = Kochen ist wichtig und dauert noch an*) / have you cooked (☺ III p25/1, *Resultat: strange smell*)
41. have been (☺ III p27, *Attention: be*)
42. Have you been waiting (☺ III p25/2, *Handlung = Warten ist wichtig*)
43. has Charlie been playing (☺ III p25/2, *Handlung und Dauer der Handlung sind wichtig, er spielt noch immer*)
44. has *always* worked (☺ II p68, ☺ III p25/1, *wiederholte Handlung*)
45. has *always* seen (☺ II p68, ☺ III p25/1, *wiederholte Handlung*, ☺ III p27 *Attention: see*)
46. has *never* been, has *always* been (☺ II p68, ☺ III p25/1 *wiederholte Handlung*)
47. have been staying (☺ III p25/2, *Handlung ist noch nicht abgeschl., sie sind noch immer in Venedig*)
48. has been driving (☺ III p25/2, *Handlung ist noch nicht abgeschlossen, sie schreit noch immer*); has been crying (☺ III p25/2, *Dauer soll betont werden*)
49. has been taking (☺ III p25/2, *Handlung ist noch nicht abgeschlossen*)
50. has been keeping (☺ III p25/2, *Handlung ist noch nicht abgeschlossen*)
51. have been (☺ III p27, *Attention:be*)
52. have been staying (☺ III p25/2, *Handlung ist noch nicht abgeschlossen*)
53. has been (☺ III p27, *Attention:be*), have known (☺ III p27, *Attention:know*)
54. have you been doing (☺ III p25/2, *Handlung ist wichtig: das Schmutzigmachen*) / have you done (☺ II p68, ☺ III p25/1, *Resultat ist wichtig: die schmutzigen Stiefel*)
55. have been trying (☺ III p25/2, *Handlung ist noch nicht abgeschlossen*)
56. have *just* managed (☺ II p89, *Resultat: Problem gelöst*)
57. has *always* had (☺ II p68, ☺ III p25/1)
58. has been wearing (☺ III p25/2, *Handlung = Tragen der Secondhand Kleidung dauert noch an*)
59. have not seen / haven't seen (☺ III p27, *Attention: see*)
60. hasn't slept (☺ III p25/1, *Resultat wichtig: he is nervous*) / hasn't been sleeping (☺ III p25/2, *Dauer wichtig*)
61. have broken (☺ II p68, ☺ III p25/1 *wiederholte Handlung:* **second** *time*)
62. has disliked (☺ III p27, *Attention: dislike*)
63. have had (☺ III p27, *Attention: have = besitzen*)
64. has refused (☺ III p27, *Attention: refuse*)
65. haven't seen (☺ III p25/1, *Resultat: nicht gesehen*), have you been doing (☺ III p25/2, *Dauer der Handlung wichtig*), have you been (☺ III p27, *Attention: be*)
66. has been sitting (☺ III p25/2, *Dauer der Handlung wichtig, Handlung noch nicht abgeschlossen = Katze sitzt noch immer*)
67. haven't been listening (☺ III p25/2, *Dauer der Hdlg. und Hdlg. = das Nichtzuhören sind wichtig*)
68. have had, has stopped (☺ II p68, ☺ III p25/1, *Kopfschmerz beendet, Resultat ist wichtig: der Schmerz ist weg*)
69. have been thinking (☺ III p25/2, *Dauer der Hdlg. wichtig, ich werde wohl noch weiterdenken müssen,* **think** *heißt hier* **nachdenken** *und nicht glauben, daher ist Dauerform möglich.*)
70. have been running (☺ III p25/2, *Dauer d. Handlung und Hdlg. selbst = running around sind wichtig*) / have run (☺ III p25/1, *Handlung = Herumlaufen beendet, Resultat: my feet hurt ist wichtiger*)
71. has not been (☺ III p27, *Attention: be*)

72. have owned (☺ III p27, *Attention: own*)
73. hasn't found (☺ II p68, *not yet*,
    has been looking for (☺ III p25/2, *Handlung = das Suchen ist noch nicht beendet*)
74. have been ringing (☺ III p25/2, *Handlung u.Dauer wichtig*), have you been (☺ III p27, *Attention: be*)
75. hasn't been going out (☺ III p25/2, *Handlung und Dauer der Handlung sind wichtig*) / hasn't gone out
76. hasn't been doing (☺ III p25/2, *Handlung und Dauer der Handlung sind wichtig*)
77. have *never* understood (☺ II p68, *never*, ☺ III p27, *Attention: understand*)
78. have rung (☺ III p25/1, *wiederh.Hdlg.: four times*)
79. have been shouting (☺ III p25/2, *Handlung und Dauer wichtig*)
80. has been (☺ III p27, *Attention: be*)
81. haven't heard (☺ III p27, *Attention: hear*)
82. hasn't hoovered (☺ III p25/1, *Resultat wichtig: They are quite dirty*), has been lying (☺ III p25/2, *Dauer d. Handlung wichtig: sie liegt noch immer mit Grippe im Bett*)
83. has been standing, have been living (☺ III p25/2, *Dauer der Handlung wichtig: Baum steht noch immer, wir wohnen dort noch immer*)
84. have sent (☺ III p26, **three** letters), hasn*'t yet* answered (☺ II p68, *not yet*)
85. has been sleeping (☺ III p25/2, *Dauer der Hdlg. wichtig: Baby schläft noch immer*)
86. has been teaching (☺ III p25/2, *Dauer der Hdlg. wichtig: unterrichtet noch immer*)
87. has belonged (☺ III p27, *Attention: belong*)
88. hasn't bought (☺ III p25/1, *Resultat wichtig: Er sieht altmodisch aus*)
89. have been looking for (☺ III p25/2, *Dauer der Handlung wichtig: wir suchen noch immer*), have not yet found (☺ II p68, *not yet*)
90. has been raining (☺ III p25/2, *Dauer der Handlung wichtig: es regnet noch immer*)
91. has been taking (☺ II p68, *recently*, ☺ III p25/2, *Handlung dauert noch immer an*)
92. has been standing (☺ III p25/2, *Dauer der Hdlg. wichtig: steht noch immer dort*)
93. have been staying (☺ III p25/2, *Dauer der Hdlg. wichtig: werden auch weiterhin dortbleiben*)
94. has been baking (☺ III p25/2, *Dauer der Handlung wichtig: sie bäckt noch welche*)
95. has baked (☺ III p25/1, *Resultat wichtig: Now she is ready.*)
96. have tried (☺ III p25/1, *wiederholte Handlung: **five** times*)
97. has been looking for (☺ III p25/2, *Hdlg. wichtig*), hasn't seen (☺ III p27, *Attention: see*)
98. has been getting (☺ III p25/2, *Handlung und Dauer wichtig: sie ist noch immer dort*), has been (☺ III p27, *Attention: be*)
99. have been building (☺ III p25/2, *Handlung und Dauer wichtig: sie wird noch immer gebaut*)
100. has been raining (☺ III p25/2, *Handlung und Dauer wichtig: es regnet noch immer*), haven't been able to/have been unable to (☺II p89)
101. have studied (☺ III p25/1, *Resultat wichtig: Now I know them.*)
102. have wanted (☺ III p27, *Attention: want*)
103. has adored (☺ III p27, *Attention: adore*)
104. has been having (☺ III p25/1, *Dauer der Handlung wichtig: Handlung dauert weiter an*)
105. has been trying (☺ III p25/2, *Dauer der Handlung wichtig: Handlung dauert weiter an*)
106. hasn't cared (☺ III p27, *Attention: care*)
107. has refused (☺ III p27, *Attention: refuse*), have known (☺ III p27, *Attention: know*)
108. has always been (☺ III p25/1, *wiederholte Hdlg.*), has been (☺ III p27, *Attention: be*)
109. has been trying (☺ III p25/2, *Dauer soll betont werden: the whole afternoon*)
110. have you been doing (☺ III p25/2, *Handlung soll betont werden*)

page 33

*Da es sich um ein **Telefongepräch** handelt und **Linda** sich noch am Urlaubsort befindet und deshalb alle Handlungen besonders **wichtig** sind und **noch andauern**, ziehen wir hier die **progressive** form vor.*

Linda: have been having
 have been (☺ III p27, *Attention: be*)
Pam: Have you been snorkelling?
Linda: have been diving
 have been playing
Pam: have you found (☺ II p68, *yet*, ☺ III p25/1)
 have you been doing
Linda: have been having
 have been talking
 have been lying
 have been getting
 have been sailing
 have been going
Pam: have you been doing
Linda: have been (☺ III p27, *Attention: be*)
 have been running
 (have been) walking
 have been holding
Pam: Has he tri**ed** (☺ II p68, *yet*, ☺ III p25/1)
Linda: have been kissing
 have been (☺ III p27, *Attention: be*)

pages 40, 41, 42, 43, 44

1. heavily (*Seite 34 Regel a*)
2. easily (*Seite 34 Regel a*)
3. aggressive (*is ist ein Hilfsverb, daher kein Adverb*)
4. furiously (*Seite 34 Regel a*)
5. slow (*are ist Hilfsverb*)
6. early (*early hat nur eine Form für Adjektiv und Adverb, Seite 35*)
7. slowly (*Seite 34 Regel a*)
8. quietly (34a)
9. quietly (*die ing-form gilt als Verb,* 34a)
10. wonderful (39)
11. interesting (39)
12. pretty awfully (37/34c)

13. difficult (*is ist Hilfsverb*)
14. pretty good (37/34b)
15. clearly, slowly (34a)
16. hardly (36)
17. nearly (36)
18. well (36)
19. perfectly (34a)
20. perfect (*is ist Hilfsverb*)
21. fine (*feel fine = sich wohlfühlen*)
22. bad (*bad ist Adjektiv, zwischen Artikel u. Hptwort*)
23. good (39)
24. fast (36) / quickly (34a)
25. quiet (*be ist Hilfsverb*), carefully (34a)
26. well (36)
27. in a friendly way (36)
28. tired (39)
29. good (*is ist Hilfsverb*), well (36)
30. terribly badly (34c)
31. extrem**e**ly cold (34b/35)
32. fairly good (37/34b)
33. fair, good (*is ist Hilfsverb*)
34. fairly well (34c/37)
35. good (39)
36. awfully (34b)
37. cheap (*are ist Hilfsverb*)
38. fresh, good (39)
39. good (39)
40. bad (*was ist Hilfsverb*), badly (34a)
41. well (34a/36)
42. sadly (34a)
43. happ**i**ly (34a/35)
44. nice, friendly (*is ist Hilfsverb*),
    in a friendly way / manner / fashion (36)
45. daily (35)
46. quickly, carefully (34a)
47. good (*is* ist Hilfsverb), well (36)
48. cold (39), hot (*Adjektiv: Artikel und Hauptwort*)
49. awful (39)
50. friendly (*Adjektiv: Art. u. Hptwort*), quickly (34a)
51. good (39), salty (*is ist Hilfsverb*)
52. well (36/34a)
53. beautifully (34a)
54. slow (*are ist Hilfsverb*), quickly (34a)
55. fast (36), excellent (*is ist Hilfsverb*)
56. angrily (39 *exceptions*)
57. badly (34a)
58. pretty (39)
59. carefully (34a), difficult (*is ist Hilfsverb*),
    easily (34a)
60. politely (34a)
61. angry (39)
62. badly (34a), angry (39), easily (34b)
63. carelessly (34a)
64. awful (39)
65. in a silly way / manner / fashion (36)
66. fair (37)
67. nearly (36), deep (*Adjektiv: Artikel u.Hauptwort*)
68. deeply (37)
69. lately (36)
70. hardly (36), good (*Adjektiv: Artikel u.Hauptwort*)
71. highly (37)
72. near, nearly (36)
73. in a silly way / manner / fashion (36)
74. hard (36)
75. horrible (39)
76. well (36/34a)
77. busy (*is ist Hilfsverb*)
78. quickly (34a), terrible (39)
79. heavily (34a)
80. badly, quickly (34a)
81. nervous (*are ist Hilfsverb*), carefully (34a)
82. cheap / cheaply (38)
83. hardly, hard (36)
84. busily (34a), tired (*am ist Hilfsverb*), quickly (34a)
85. beautifully (34a)
86. clearly (34a)
87. hard (36), badly (34a)
88. happily (39 *exceptions*),
    nice (*Adjektiv: Artikel und Hauptwort*)
89. loud(ly) (38), quietly, slowly (34a)
90. well (34a/36), good (*Adjektiv: Art. u. Hauptwort*)
91. in a friendly way / manner / fashion (36)
92. terribly stupid (34b)
93. horribly expensive (34b)
94. pretty badly (34c), free (37)
95. final**ly** (34a),
    correct (*Adjektiv: Artikel u. Hauptwort*), shyly (35)
96. completely (34b)
97. totally (34b) (*in love = verliebt, gilt als Adjektiv und wird näher bestimmt*)
98. happily (34a), freely (34a)
99. fantastic**ally** (34a/35)
100. extrem**e**ly (34b)
101. early (35), late (36)
102. in a lovely way / manner / fashion (36)
103. low (*Adjektiv: Artikel und Hauptwort*)
104. nearly (36)
105. late (36)
106. fairly well (34c/37), quickly (34a)
107. direct (37)
108. directly (37)
109. high (37)
110. highly (37/34b)
111. deeply (37)
112. closely (37)
113. dearly (37)
114. readily (37)
115. short (37), quickly (34a)
116. highly (37), bad (*bestimmt d. Hptwort*)
117. deep (37)
118. closely (37)
119. dear (37)
120. completely (34b)
121. straight (36)
122. low (36),
123. doubtless (36), deeply (37)
124. closely (37)
125. deep (37)
126. dear (37)
127. freely (37)
128. prettily (37), elegant (39), short (37),
    admiringly (39, *exceptions*)
129. in a silly way / manner / fashion (36)
130. Shortly (37)
131. readily (37)
132. close / closer (37)
133. dearly (37)
134. free (37)
135. just (37, just = gerade + pres.perf.), terribly (34b)
136. Just (37)

137. pretty (37)
138. highly (38)
139. seriously (34a), carefully (34a)
140. slow (38), incorrectly (38), sharp(ly) (38)
141. pretty false (37)
142. closely (37)
143. direct (37)
144. long (*Adjektiv: Artikel u. Hauptwort*),
    silent (39, *remain*)
145. curiously (39, *exceptions*), pale (39, *turn*)
146. famous (39, *become*)
147. difficult (39), perfectly (34a)

page 46

1. more quickly (page 45/1), longer (45/2)
2. faster (45/2) / more quickly (45/1)
3. earlier (45/2), longer (45/2)
4. more heavily (45/1)
5. in a friendlier way (45/2)
6. more carefully (45/1)
7. best (45/3)
8. faster (45/2), higher (45/2)
9. more severely (45/1)
10. more beautifully (45/1)
11. fairest (45/2)
12. harder (45/2), more easily (45/1)
13. better (45/3)
14. higher (45/2)
15. more slowly (45/1)
16. more carefully (45/1)
17. more heavily (45/1)
18. more silently (45/1)
19. more elegantly (45/1)
20. more carefully (45/1) and
    slower (38, *drive slow*)
21. better (45/3)

pages 47, 48, 49, 50, 51

1. more carefully (☺ III p45/1)
2. cleverer (☺ II p 33/b; ☺ III p39, *be*;
   ☺ II p52, *Attention*)
3. better (☺ III p45/3)
4. more tired (☺ II p35/b; ☺ III p39, *be*;
   ☺ II p52, *Attention*),
   harder (☺ III p36, p45/2)
5. more careful (☺ II p34/2a; ☺ III p39, *be*;
   ☺ II p52, *Attention*),
   last (☺ II p37)
6. worse (☺ II p35/3; ☺ III p39, *be*;
   ☺ II p52, *Attention*)
7. thinner (☺ II p33/a, ☺ III p39, *look*)
8. cheaper (☺ III p39, *be*; ☺ II p52, *Attention*)
9. more painful (☺ II p34/2a *wie: careful*;
   ☺ III p39, *be*; ☺ II p52, *Attention*)
10. next, last (☺ II p37)
11. more busily (☺ III p34/a, 45/1)
12. thinnest (☺ II p33/a, ☺ III p39, *be*;
    ☺ II p52, *Attention*)
13. more politely (☺ III p45/1),
    friendlier (☺ II p34 *wie: happy*),
    nicer (☺ II p33/a), better (☺ III p45/3)
14. best (☺ II p35/3)
15. more quickly (☺ III p45/1)
16. least (☺ III p45/3)
17. more slowly (☺ III p45/1; p38)
18. more successfully (☺ III p45/1)
19. better (☺ III p45/3), more seriously (☺ III p45/1)
20. latest (☺ II p37), more exciting (☺ II p35/c),
    last (☺ II p37)
21. better (☺ II p35/3; ☺ III p39),
    best (☺ II p35/3)
22. carefully / more carefully (☺ III p45/1)
23. louder / more loudly (☺ III p38)
24. worse (☺ II p35/3; ☺ III p39, *get*)
25. happier (☺ II p34; ☺ III p39, *be*; ☺ II p52,
    Attention), more charming (*wie:* ☺ II p35/b)
26. better (☺ III p45/3)
27. harder (☺ III p36, *hard;* ☺ III p45/2),
    better (☺ II p35/3)
28. more prettily (☺ III p45/1; p37)
29. more heavily (☺ III p45/1)
30. further (☺ II p36)
31. most quickly (☺ III p45/1)
32. more fluently (☺ III p45/1)
33. further (☺ II p36)
34. nicer (☺ III p39, *smell,* ☺ II p33a)
35. more cautiously (☺ III p39, *exceptions*)
36. more beautiful (☺ III p39, *look*),
    better (☺ III p45/3)
37. better (☺ III p45/3), more clearly (☺ III p45/1),
    and more slowly (☺ III p38)
38. most exciting (*bestimmt ein Hauptwort: pictures
    näher, nicht ein Verb. Ist Adjektiv!*) (☺II p35c),
    greatest (*bestimmt ein Hauptwort: artist näher,
    nicht ein Verb. Ist Adjektiv!*)
39. most quickly (☺ III p45/1)
40. more sadly (☺ III p39, *exceptions*; p45/1)
41. worse (☺ III p45/3), better (☺ II p35/3)
42. most good-looking (☺ II p35/c)
43. more awful (☺ III p39, *smell*; ☺ II p34/2a)
44. worst (☺ II p35/3)
45. more (☺ III p45/3)
46. worse, worse (☺ II p35/3, ☺ III p39, *get*)
47. most terrible (*wie:* ☺ II p35/c)
48. best (☺ II p35/3)
49. most frightening (☺ II p35/c)
50. more horribly (☺ III p45/1)
51. happiest (☺ II p34)
52. most loudly / loudest (☺ III p38, *we speak
    loud(ly)*)
53. harder (☺ III p45/2; p36)
54. worse (☺ III p45/3)
55. hungrier (☺ III p39, *feel*)
56. more dangerous (*wie:* ☺ II p35/c)
57. worst (☺ II p35/3),
    easiest (☺ II p34, *bestimmt ein Hauptwort:
    exercises näher, nicht ein Verb. Ist daher
    Adjektiv!*)
58. further (☺ II p36)
59. more quickly and clearly (☺ III p45/1),
    fast (☺ II p39: *as .... as mit Grundstufe*)
60. harder (☺ III p36), more (☺ III p45/3)
61. more expensive (*wie:* ☺ II p35/c)
62. more easily (☺ III p34/b; p45/1)
63. more greedily (☺ III p34/a, ☺ III p45/1)
64. nicest (☺ II p33/a)
65. more carefully (☺ III p45/1),
    better (☺ II p35/3)

66. last (☺ II p37),
    more boring (☺ II p35/b)
67. most terrible (wie: ☺ II p35/c)
68. worst (☺ II p35/3)
69. more easily (☺ III p45/1),
    more expensive (wie: ☺ II p35/c)
70. more selfishly (☺ III p45/1),
    bigger / biggest (☺ II p33/1a)
71. more colourfully (☺ III p45/1)
72. better (☺ III p45/3),
    taller and slimmer (wie: ☺ II p33/1a)
73. more nervous (☺ III p39, *feel*, wie: ☺ II p35/b),
    easier (☺ III p38, ☺ II p34)
74. deeper (☺ III p37),
    less (☺ II p35/3),
    fresh (☺ III p39, *feel*)
75. cheaper / more cheaply (☺ III p38)
76. closer (☺ III p37),
    more quickly (☺ III p45/1)
77. most frightening (☺ II p35/c)
78. more believable (☺ III p39, *seem*)
79. more nicely (☺ III p45/1)
80. earlier (☺ III p35)
81. more fantastic**ally** (☺ III p35, p45/1)
82. most patient (wie: ☺ II p35/2b)
83. worse (☺ III p45/3)
84. most awful (☺ II p34/2a)
85. best (☺ II p35/3)
86. more quickly (☺ III p45/1)
87. worst (☺ II p35/3)
88. deepest (☺ III p37)
89. most interesting and most exciting (☺ II p35/2c)
90. faster (☺ III p45/2),
    more dangerously (☺ III p45/1)
91. last (☺ II p37)
92. nicer (wie: ☺ II p33/a),
    more helpful (wie: ☺ II p34/2a),
    friendlier (☺ II p34 wie *lovely*)
93. fairer (☺ III p37)
94. more freely (☺ III p37; p45/1)
95. dearer (☺ III p37)
96. more incorrectly (☺ III p45/1)
97. slower / more slowly (☺ III p38)
98. softer (☺ III p39, *feel*)
99. pleasanter (☺ III p39, *sound*; ☺ II p34/c)
100. longer (☺ III p38)
101. greater (☺ III p39, *sound*),
     more realistic (wie: ☺ II p35/c)
102. slower (☺ III p38),
     later (☺ II p37)
103. more prettily (☺ III p37, p45/1)
104. warmer (☺ III p39, *get*)
105. best (☺ III p45/3)
106. more carefully (☺ III p39, *exceptions*; p45/1)
107. angrier (☺ II p34, wie *lovely*)
108. least (☺ III p45/3),
     stronger (☺ II p33/a)
109. more appropriately (☺ III p35, p45/1)
110. more intensely (☺ III p45/1)
111. most intelligently (☺ III p45/1)
112. longer (☺ III p38, p45/2)
113. more quietly (☺ III p45/1)
114. in a friendlier way (☺ III p45/2)
115. less (☺ II p35/3, *less = Adjektiv, bestimmt: meat*)
116. busier (☺ II p34, wie *happy*)

page 53

1. The longer he had to wait, the sa**dd**er he became.
2. The more she read about it, the less she understood.
3. The faster / the more quickly you work, the sooner you'll be ready.
4. The more expensive the jeans are, the better they fit.
5. The less you sleep, the more tired you are.
6. The more you smoke, the worse you feel.
7. The more make-up you use, the worse (it is) for your skin.
8. The louder / The more loudly (☺ III p38, *wie speak loud(ly)*) they cried, the more nervous she got.
9. The unhappier she is, the fa**tt**er she gets.
10. The faster / the more quickly he runs, the more exhausted he is.
11. The more helpful you are, the more friends you'll have.
12. The longer she stays at home with her children, the better for them. (☺ III p38, *stay long*)
13. The faster / The more quickly you eat, the worse (it is) for your stomach.
14. The longer I was watching the picture, the more beautiful it seemed to me.
15. The angrier he got, the more I laughed.
16. The more wildly he danced, the sicker she felt / she got.
17. The more he drank, the worse his headache got.
18. The more quickly / The faster he drove, the more dangerous it became.
19. The friendlier the doctor is, the more patients visit him.
20. The more carefully you study, the easier the exam will be for you.
21. The more jealous you are, the worse for your friendship.
22. The healthier you are, the happier you are.
23. The more you read, the better you will become at German.
24. The more accurately you work, the more beautiful your silk scarf will be.
25. The more you watch TV, the worse for your eyes.
26. The cheekier he is, the less the other children like him.
27. The more often you tidy your room, the more comfortable it is.
28. The more horrible / terrible / awful the film is, the more frightened you will be later.
29. The worse his marks are, the more he hates school.
30. The more often you practise the recorder, the better you are able to / you can play.
31. The more stains there are on your trousers, the dirtier **they** look.
32. The friendlier you are, the better people like you.
33. The more beautiful the weather is, the happier people are.
34. The more chocolate you eat, the worse (it is) for your teeth.
35. The more arrogant he is, the less help he gets.
36. The more often your pencil falls down on / onto the floor, the more often it breaks.
37. The bi**gg**er the flat (is), the better for the children.
38. The more flowers grow in the garden, the nicer it looks.
39. The more you worry, the worse for your health.

page 59

*Es gibt meistens **mehrere** Lösungsmöglichkeiten, um „werden" zu übersetzen. Die gebräuchlicheren sind hier angeführt:*

1. Nowadays **more and more** children are learning French and Spanish.
2. Jim finds tennis **less and less interesting**.
3. He is able to jump **higher and higher**.
4. The guests were singing **louder and louder / more and more loudly** (☺ III p38, *wie speak loud(ly)*)
5. Ann is eating **less and less**.
6. Tom is eating **fewer and fewer** sweets.
7. How about your headache? – It is *getting / becoming* **better and better**.
8. It is *getting / becoming* **more and more difficult** to find a good friend, Lucy thinks.
9. Tom is **more and more interested** in computers.
10. The weather is *getting / becoming* **colder and colder**.
11. His health is *getting / becoming* **worse and worse**.
12. He met her **more and more often**.
13. It is *getting / becoming* **darker and darker**. I think we should leave now.
14. Bill liked Mandy **better and better**.
15. Peter is working **more and more diligently**.
16. It is *getting / becoming* **later and later** and we are still here!
17. My foot hurt **more and more severely**.
18. His father drank **more and more**.
19. Mr Miller complains that the children are *getting / becoming* **cheekier and cheekier**.
20. His problems are *getting / becoming* **bigger and bigger**.
21. His girlfriends are *becoming / getting* **younger and younger** the older he *grows / gets / becomes*.
22. The screams were *getting / becoming* **louder and louder**.
23. The poor are *getting / becoming* **poorer and poorer**, the rich **richer and richer**.
24. The old hits are *getting / becoming* **more and more popular**.
25. The prices for bananas are *getting / becoming* **higher and higher**.
26. He promised her **more and more**, but, nevertheless (☺ II p 63), she left him.
27. She comes home **later and later**.
28. Her face *went / turned* **paler and paler**.
29. I am *getting* **colder and colder**.
30. She *went* **crazier and crazier**.
31. Mr Smith *grew / was growing / got / was getting / became / was becoming* **angrier and angrier**.
32. It is *getting / becoming* **more and more expensive** going abroad.
33. Mother is *getting / becoming* **more and more nervous**.
34. We are *growing* **older and older and wiser and wiser**.
35. She *went / turned* **redder and redder** in the face.
36. Mrs Austin *went* **blinder and blinder**.

pages 61, 62, 63

1. had seen, was
2. went, had been
3. had left, was
4. had watched, gave
5. had had, went
6. had read, called
7. could not / was not able to / was unable to, had broken
8. had reached, began
9. went, had finished
10. had turned, couldn't / was not able to / was unable to
11. had hidden, couldn't / was not able to / was unable to
12. had been, missed
13. was, had laughed
14. had packed, called, went
15. hurried, had done
16. had eaten, drank
17. had worked, became
18. had missed, had to
19. took, had done
20. were, had worked
21. had lived, emigrated
22. left, saw, had forgotten
23. began, had read
24. had already died, arrived
25. entered, found, had already left
26. had sung, applauded
27. felt, had slept
28. had shouted, was
29. saw, had read
30. arrived, had already left
31. did not watch, had seen
32. got, had already started
33. came, noticed, had stolen
34. heard, knew, had happened
35. passed, had worked
36. knew, had seen
37. had been, did
38. were, had wasted
39. told, had left
40. told, had asked
41. couldn't / was not able to / was unable to, had lost
42. had written, bought, ran, posted
43. had broken, could / were able to
44. had recognised, ran, could
45. had lost, was
46. had never met, didn't recognise
47. was not, had just had
48. wanted, couldn't / were not able to / were unable to, had already bought
49. did not get, had eaten up
50. was, had done
51. did not want, had broken
52. wanted, had left
53. smoked, had finished
54. had disappeared, had to
55. had just closed, set
56. could / was able to, had already slipped

page 64

1. had been allowed to, had to
2. had not been able to / had been unable to
3. had had to, could / was able to
4. had been allowed to, had to
5. had been able to
6. had not been allowed to
7. had not had to / hadn't had to
8. had already been able to
9. had had to

pages 66, 67, 68

1. will go / 'll go (☺ III p7/2, *bestimmte Situation*)
2. would have helped (☺ III p65/2) / would help (☺ III p65/1)
3. will run (☺ III p7/2, *bestimmte Situation*)
4. would succeed (☺ III p9)
5. turns (☺ III p7/1, *allgemeingültige Aussage, Tatsache, Naturgesetz*)
6. weren't / wasn't (*spoken English*) (☺ III p9)
7. will catch (☺ III p7/2, *bestimmte Situation*)
8. could / would be able to (☺ III p9)
9. would have asked (☺ III p65/2)
10. gets (☺ III p7/1, *er wird immer zornig*) will get (☺ III p7/2, *bestimmte Situation*)
11. are (☺ III p7/1, *Bitte, Aufforderung*)
12. had had (☺ III p65/2)
13. can (☺ III p7/2, *best.Sit.*) / 7/1 (*immer*)
14. were / was (*spoken English*) (☺ III p9)
15. must / will have to (☺ III p7/2, *best. Situation*), (must = have to, ☺ II p7)
16. would have taken (☺ III p65/2) / would take (☺ III p65/1)
17. can (☺ III p7/2, *best.Sit.*) / 7/1 (*immer*) (*can : hier im Sinn von dürfen, daher passt die Ersatzform can = to be able to, fähig sein, <u>nicht</u>*) (☺ III p20)
18. would help (☺ III p9)
19. would have been (☺ III p65/2)
20. breaks (☺ III p7/1, *das ist immer so, Naturgesetz*)
21. went (☺ III p9)
22. will not bite / won't bite (☺ III p7/2, *best. Sit.*)
23. will scratch (☺ III p7/2, *bestimmte Situation*)
24. were / was (*spoken English*) (☺ III p9)
25. would have met (☺ III p65/2)
26. must (☺ III p7/1, *Bitte, Aufforderung*)
27. would be (☺ III p65/1)
28. had not had / hadn't had (☺ III p65/2)
29. would have frozen (☺ III p65/2)
30. smothers (☺ III p7/1, *das ist immer so, Naturges.*)
31. could / would be able to (☺ III p65/1)
32. must / will have to (☺ III p7/2, *best. Situation*) (must = have to, ☺ II p7)
33. had put on (☺ III p65/2)
34. will sting (☺ III p7/2, *bestimmte Situation*) / stings (☺ III p7/1, *Tatsache, Naturgesetz*)
35. would not have invited (☺ III p65/2)
36. will go (☺ III p7/2, *bestimmte Situation*)
37. can / are able to (☺ III p7/2, *bestimmte Situation*)
38. would have been able to buy / could have bought (☺ III p65/2)
39. would not have / wouldn't have (☺ III p65/1)
40. would laugh (☺ III p9)
41. cannot / can't / won't be able to (☺ III p7/2, *bestimmte Situation*)
42. had not come / hadn't come (☺ III p65/2)
43. would be / 'd be (☺ III p65/1)
44. could not have passed / would not have been able to pass (☺ III p65/2) / would not be able to pass (☺ III p65/1)
45. had looked (☺ III p65/2)
46. would be / 'd be (☺ III p9)
47. had known (☺ III p65/2)
48. tell (☺ III p7/1, *Bitte, Aufforderung*)
49. gets (☺ III p7/1, *Tatsache, Naturgesetz*)
50. would have walked (☺ III p65/2)
51. went (☺ III p9)
52. always feels (☺ III p7/1, *Tatsache, das ist immer so bei ihm*)
53. have (☺ III p7/1, *Tatsache, Naturgesetz*)
54. did not shine (☺ III p9)
55. would not stay (☺ III p65/1) / would not have stayed (☺ III p65/2)
56. will phone (☺ III p7/2, *bestimmte Situation*)
57. had known (☺ III p65/2)
58. would not be / wouldn't be (☺ III p65/1)
59. will say (☺ III p7/2, *bestimmte Situation*)
60. had stayed up (☺ III p65/1)
61. will go (☺ III p7/2, *bestimmte Situation*)
62. will you have (☺ III p7/2, *bestimmte Situation*)
63. weren't / wasn't (*spoken English*) (☺ III p9)
64. do not find / don't find (☺ III p7/2, *best. Situation*)
65. will forgive (☺ III p7/2, *bestimmte Situation*)
66. skids (☺ III p7/1, *Tatsache, Naturgesetz, das ist immer so*)
67. would know (☺ III p65/1)
68. failed (☺ III p9)
69. wags (☺ III p7/1, *Tatsache, Naturgesetz, das ist immer so*)
70. would be / 'd be (☺ III p9)
71. would not have been able to / would have been unable to (☺ III p65/2)
72. changes (☺ III p7/1, *Tatsache, Naturgesetz, das ist immer so*)
73. kept (☺ III p9)
74. rolls (☺ III p7/1, *Tatsache, Naturgesetz, das ist immer so*)
75. would not go (☺ III p9)
76. melts (☺ III p7/1, *Tatsache, Naturgesetz, das ist immer so*)
77. would not have asked (☺ III p65/2)
78. would sit (☺ III p65/1)
79. would not have had to / wouldn't have had to (☺ III p65/2) / wouldn't have to (☺ III p65/1)
80. see (☺ III p7/1, *Tatsache, Naturgesetz, das ist immer so*)
81. will soon feel (☺ III p7/2)
82. begins (☺ III p7/1, *Tatsache, Naturgesetz, das ist immer so*)

pages 74, 75, 76, 77

*Achtung: **Infinitive** werden **nicht** verwandelt!*

1. that ... will be (p 69/1, <u>announce</u> is in present, no change of tenses)
2. that Paris had been (p 69/2)
3. that ... were waiting (p 69/2)
4. that Susan didn't like (p 69/2)
5. that *she* has been working (p 69/1, p 72/6)
6. that *she* didn't smoke and that *she* was not (p 69/2, p 72/6)
7. that *she* couldn't come to *your / my / our* party (p 69/2, p 72/6) <u>because</u> *she* must take / had to take / would have to take (p 70/3)
8. that *he* had never seen (p 69/2, p 72/6)
9. that *she* was going to spend ... *her* (p 69/2, p 72/6)
10. that *he* would have ... *then* (p 69/2, p 72/6)
11. that Peter would like to have (p 70/3)
12. that *we / they* should leave *then* (p 70/3, p 72/6) <u>because</u> it was (p 69/2)
13. that *we / they* had better tell *her friend / Sue* (p 73 / *Attention* 2) ... *then* (p 70/3, p 72/6)
14. that *we / they* might be (p 70/3, p 72/6)
15. that *he* couldn't send / had not been able to send / had been unable to send (p 70/3), had been closed (p 69/2)
16. that *we* would have to repair ... (p 70/3) *the following* summer (p 72/6)
17. that if *he* had ... *he* would go (p 72/4, p 72/6)
18. will arrive ... so there *is* (p 69/1)
19. that *we / they* ought to send (p 70/3, p 72/6)
20. that *I* (p 73 / *Attention* 1) would have (p 69/2) ... for all *my* (p 73 / *Attention* 1) friends
21. that *his friend / the man / uncle Ben* ... (p 73 / *Attention* 2) had shown *him* (p 69/2)
22. <u>because</u> / that Sam had been ... <u>and that</u> he had even helped *her* carry *her* bags (p 69/2, p 72/6)
23. that *the following week she* was flying ... and was going to visit (p 69/2, p 72/6)
24. that *he* had been waiting ... but that she hadn't turned up (p 69/2, p 72/6)
25. that it was (p 69/2)
26. that *he* had returned *the day before* <u>and</u> that it had been really ... and that *he* was (p 69/2, p 72/6)
27. that the dinosaurs died out (p 72/5)
28. that if *we / they* had maps, *we / they* could find (p 72/4, p 72/6)
29. that Ben was trying to breed ... and then *Ben* (p 73 / *Att.*2) wanted to sell (p 69/2)
30. that *she* couldn't stay ... and that *she* didn't like (p 69/2, p 72/6)
31. that too ... isn't (p 72/5) healthy for *my* (p 72/6)
32. that one day *they* will find (p 69/1, p 72/6)
33. had escaped ... and had spread ... and (that) it had been awful and (that) *he* couldn't sleep / wasn't able to sleep / hadn't been able to sleep / had been unable to sleep (p 69/2, p 70/3, p 72/6)
34. that *he* (p 72/6) could see / was able to see / had been able to see (p 70/3), had been (p 69/2)
35. that shortly ... could hear / were able to hear / had been able to hear (p 70/3)
36. that *she* had got (p 69/2, p 72/6)
37. that Sally's story was ... <u>because</u> *he* knew ... and *he* couldn't believe that *her husband / Mr Miller* (p 73 / *Attention* 2) had really shouted (p 69/2)
38. that *my* complaint was (p 69/2, p 72/6)
39. that if *he* lived ..., *he* would go (p 72/4, p 72/6)
40. that the earth is (p 72/5)
41. that *they* were trying to find (p 69/2, p 72/6)
42. that Lucy spent ... and that *the day before* she had bought ... and that *he* didn't know what to do (p 69/2, p 72/6)
43. that *I* had better take ... <u>because</u> it might rain (p 70/3)
44. that *she* had been ... and that *she* had had (p 69/2)
45. that *she* hadn't quite understood (p 69/2, p 72/6)
46. that *she* will soon be able to speak (p 69/1, p 72/6)
47. that if *he* were *me*, *he* wouldn't spend (p 72/4, p 72/6)
48. *he* had listened ... *he* had gone (p 69/2, p 72/6)
49. *he* didn't know why *the man / the stranger / Tom* (p 73 / *Attention* 2) had been ... to *him* (p 69/2, p 72/6)
50. sets (p 72/5)
51. that *he* couldn't come *that night* (p 69/2, p 72/6), because *he* must finish / had to finish / would have to finish *his* (p 70/3, p 69/2, p 72/6) but that *he* could come / would be able to come (p 70/3, p 72/6) ... *the next / the following day* (p 72/6)
52. that Austria is (p 69/1)
53. that *he* had run ... but (that) *the man / Bill / his friend* had caught *him* ... and had thrown ... into *his* face (p 69/2, p 72/6)
54. that most ... spoke ... and that they had understood everything *he* had said (p 69/2, p 72/6)
55. that *she* had ... to cook the meal *then* and (that) *she* would be late *that night*. <u>She said that</u> Tony had phoned *her* and had asked *her* to help him translate (p 69/2, p 72/6)
56. that *I / you / we* mustn't watch (p 70/3, p 72/6)
57. that *she* would go ... *that* afternoon <u>and she said that</u> if *I / we / you* needed anything *she* would get it for *me / us / you*. (p 69/2, p 72/6)
58. that *they* had been having (p 69/2, p 72/6)
59. that *I / we / you* would soon know that *I was / we were / you were* ... it would be (p 69/2, p 72/6)
60. that *he* had never been ... <u>and that</u> *he* would like to spend *his* (p 69/2, p 72/6)
61. that *she* didn't want ... <u>and that</u> *she* wanted to keep *her* (p 69/2, p 72/6)
62. that *she* would arrive (p 69/2, p 72/6) ... and that *she* would be very glad if *I* picked *her* up (p 72/4, p 72/6)
63. that three years *before he* had been ... <u>and that</u> *he* had really been impressed <u>and that</u> *he* was going to come again with *his* family *that* year. (p69/2, p72/6)
64. that if the weather *were* (p 9, *Attention*) fine *the next day / the following day*, *we / they* would make (p 69/2, p 72/6)
65. that *I* mustn't play (p 70/3) ... *then* because it was too late ... would complain if *I* made (p 69/2, p 72/6)
66. that *I* didn't have to help (☺ II p7) *her* with ... <u>because</u> *she* had already had ... and it wasn't (p 69/2, p 72/6)

67. that *he* was very sorry, but *that* was *his* last word and *he* didn't want to talk (p 69/2, p 72/6)
68. that / <u>because</u> she was feeling ... *that day* <u>and</u> that it was good to be (p 69/2, p 72/6)
69. that *he* had gone ... <u>and</u> that *they* had been looking ... It had been ... and Pit had fallen ... <u>and that</u> *Pit* / *his friend* (p 73 / *Att*.2) had lost his ... and that *they* had had to find *their* way ... It had taken *them* (p 69/2, p 72/6) ... to get ...
70. that *she* would never run ... *her* parents had had ... and *she* didn't want (p 69/2, p 72/6)
71. that *he* couldn't play ... with *me that day* because *he* had hurt *his* knee. (p 69/2, p 72/6)
72. that *he* couldn't believe it was true that she had left (p 69/2, p 72/6) *his friend* (p 73 / *Att*.2) <u>because</u> *his friend* had been ... and *he* / *his friend* had loved (p 69/2, p 72/6, p 73 / Attention 2)
73. that *he* had never seen (p 69/2, p 72/6)
74. that *she* had had to go ... *the previous week* and that *she* had almost missed (p 69/2, p 72/6)
75. that *I* couldn't wear ... *that day* <u>because</u> *I* knew that ... was very (p 69/2, p 72/6)
76. that *he* must learn / had to learn / would have to learn (p70/3) to get rid of *his* aggressiveness (p72/6)
77. that *he* had been in *his* office. Suddenly *he* had had ... It had been a man who had died two years *before*. (p 69/2, p 72/6)
78. that *she* was (p 69/2, p 72/6)... and so *I* / *we* / *you* didn't have to be scared. (☺ II p7)
79. that *we* / *they* ought to tidy (p 70/3) ... *our* / *their* parents came back. (p 69/2, p 72/6)
80. that *we* / *they* had been thinking of selling *our* / *their* ... but *we* / *they* had decided to keep it ... (p 69/2, p 72/6)
81. that if Sally weren't so ... *he* would ask her to marry *him*. (p 72/4, p 72/6)
82. that *she* must / would have to speak to *her* (p70/3) after *her friend* (p 73 / *Attention* 2) had finished *her* work. (p 69/2, p 72/6)
83. that the most important thing ... had been never to give up (p 69/2)
84. that *I* / *we* / *you* could do it if *I* / *we* / *you* only tried. (p 69/2, p 72/6)
85. that *I* was allowed to see *his* ... if *I* liked. (p 69/2, p 72/6)
86. that *he* liked *his* dolls better (p 69/2, p 72/6)
87. that Rick was going to spend ... with *us* / *them* <u>because</u> *he* was flying ... than *he* had expected. (p 69/2, p 72/6)
88. that in ... there is (p 72/5)
89. that *he* had been smoking ... *he* had got (p 69/2, p 72/6)
90. that Nancy's husband was ... who was talking (p 69/2, p 72/6)
91. that *they* / *his guests* / *his friends* would be *there* soon <u>and</u> that *they* were going to have (p 69/2, p 72/6)
92. that *he* would come as soon as *he* could (p 69/2, p 72/6), but *we* / *I* didn't have to wait (☺ II p7) for *him*.
93. that *I* / *we* / *you* mustn't cross (p 70/3) ... *there*. (p 72/6)
94. that *she* would not do *that* if *she* were in *my* place. (p 72/4, p 72/6)
95. that *I* must decide / would have to decide for *myself* what *I* was going to do. (p 70/3, p 69/2, p 72/6)
96. that when *he* came round *in two days' time*, he would bring *me* ... he had borrowed from *me the previous week* <u>and</u> *he* said / promised that *he* wouldn't forget it. (p 69/2, p 72/6)
97. that *she* can't live with *him* ... because *they* are (p 69/1, p 72/6)
98. that Lucy might have to stay ... <u>because</u> *she* had got ... <u>and</u> so *we* / *they* must start / had to start / would have to start ... (p 70/3)
99. that all ... should keep (p 70/3)
100. that mass is (p 72/5)
101. that *he* had been waiting (p 69/2, p 72/6)
102. that *she* has finished *that* (p 69/1, p 72/6)
103. that *he* had last seen her ... weeks *before* (p 69/2, p 72/6)
104. that the Danube flows (p 72/5)
105. that if Brian came to *her* party, *she* would be surprised. (p 72/4, 72/6)
106. that *we* didn't have to stay (☺ II p7) ... if *we* didn't like. (p 69/2, p 72/6)
107. that *I* must be back ... (p 69/1)
108. that *he* will try ... for *our* ... when *he* is (p 69/1, p 72/6)
109. that if *she* were (p 9 / *Attention*) late, *I* / *you* / *we* must / had to / would have to put (p 70/3, p 72/6)
110. that *I* was allowed to watch ... there was (p 69/2, p 72/6)

pages 82, 83, 84, 85

Anmerkung:
Wenn bei der Lösung im 3. u. 4. Fall das / die Relativpronomen **in Klammer** *steht / stehen, kann es / können sie auch* **ausgelassen** *werden.*

1. (whom / who / that) (p 78/1 *4. Fall*)
2. whose (p 78/1 *2. Fall*)
3. **to** whom (p 78/1 *with preposition*)
4. (which / that) (p 79/2 *4. Fall*)
5. (whom / who / that) (p 78/1 *4. Fall*)
6. which / that (p 79/2 *1. Fall*)
7. **to** which (p 79/2 *with preposition*)
8. **for** which (p 79/2 *with preposition*)
9. (which / that) ... **for** (p 79/2 *with preposition*)
10. (that) (p 80/3a *4. Fall*)
11. that (p 80/3a *1. Fall*)
12. **for** whom (p 78/1 *with preposition*)
13. (who / that) ... **for** (p 78/1 *with preposition*)
14. who / that (p 78/1 *1. Fall*)
15. (that) (p 80/3c)
16. whose (p 79/2 *2. Fall*)
17. what (p 81/5)
18. that (p 80/3b)
19. which (p 81/4)
20. What (p 81/5)
21. what (p 81/5)
22. (that) (p 80/3a)
23. (who / that) ... **to** (p 78/1 *with preposition*)
24. (that) (p 80/3b)
25. (who / that) ... **with** (p 78/1 *with preposition*)
26. (that) (p 80/3b)

27. what (p 81/5)
28. (that) (p 80/3a)
29. which (p 81/4)
30. (who / that) ... **to** (p 78/1 *with preposition*)
31. (whom / who / that) (p 78/1 *4. Fall*)
32. that (p 80/3a)
33. which (p 81/4)
34. what (p 81/5)
35. which (p 81/4)
36. what (p 81/5)
37. which (p 81/4)
38. what (p 81/5)
39. (who / that) ... **to** (p 78/1 *with preposition*)
40. What (p 81/5)
41. what (p 81/5)
42. (who / that) ... **with** (p 78/1 *with preposition*)
43. **in** which (p 79/2 *with preposition*)
44. (which / that) ... **in** (p 79/2 *with preposition*)
45. (that) (p 80/3a)
46. what (p 81/5)
47. (whom / who / that) (p 78/1 *4. Fall*)
48. what (p 81/5)
49. (that) (p 80/3a)
50. what (p 81/5)
51. (that / which) (p 79/2 *4. Fall*)
52. (which / that) ... **for** (p 79/2 *with preposition*), (that) (p 80/3b)
53. what (p 81/5)
54. what (p 81/5)
55. which / that (p 79/2 *1. Fall*)
56. (which / that) (p 79/2 *4. Fall*)
57. (that) (p 80/3a)
58. what (p 81/5)
59. (which / that) (p 79/2 *4. Fall*)
60. which (p 81/4)
61. what (p 81/5)
62. whose (p 78/1 *2. Fall*)
63. (which / that) (p 79/2 *4. Fall*)
64. what (p 81/5) *Achtung! Relativpron. bezieht sich hier nicht auf **anybody**, sondern auf **happened**!*
65. whose (p 79/2 *2. Fall*)
66. which / that (p 79/2 *1. Fall*)
67. what (p 81/5)
68. which (p 81/4)
69. (which / that) ... **from / out of** (p 79/2 *with prep.*)
70. which (p 81/4)
71. (that) (p 80/3a)
72. **in** which (p 79/2 *with preposition*)
73. (which / that) ... **in** (p 79/2 *with preposition*)
74. (who / that) ... **for** (p 78/1 *with preposition*)
75. **for** whom (p 78/1 *with preposition*)
76. which (p 81/4)
77. What (p 81/5)
78. (who / that) ... **at** (p 78/1 *with preposition*)
79. **at** whom (p 78/1 *with preposition*)
80. (which / that) (p 79/2 *4. Fall*)
81. (that) (p 80/3c)
82. which / that (p 79/2 *1. Fall*)
83. which (p 81/4)
84. (who / that) ... **of** (p 78/1 *with preposition*)
85. which (p 81/4)
86. what (p 81/5)
87. that (p 80/3a)
88. (that) (p 80/3b)
89. (that) (p 80/3a)
90. (that) (p 80/3b)
91. which (p 81/4) *Achtung! Relativpron. bezieht sich hier **nicht** auf **everything**, sondern auf **den ganzen vorherigen Satz**!*
92. whose (p 78/1 *2. Fall*)
93. (which / that) (p 79/2 *4. Fall*)
94. what (p 81/5)
95. (which / that) ... **in** (p 79/2 *with preposition*)
96. (that) (p 80/3b)
97. (who / that) ... **to** (p 78/1 *with preposition*)
98. whose (p 79/2 *2. Fall*)
99. (that) (p 80/3a)
100. who / that (p 78/1 *1. Fall*)
101. (whom / who / that) (p 78/1 *4. Fall*)
102. whose (p 78/1 *2. Fall*)
103. (which / that) (p 79/2 *4. Fall*)
104. **in / at** which (p 79/2 *with preposition*)
105. (which / that) ... **in / at** (p 79/2 *with preposition*)
106. (that) (p 80/3b)
107. (that) (p 80/3a)
108. (which / that) ... **in / at** (p 79/2 *with preposition*)
109. (that) (p 80/3a)
110. which (p 81/4)
111. which (p 81/4)
112. (that) (p 80/3a)
113. what (p 81/5)
114. **into** which (p 79/2 *with preposition*)
115. (which / that) ... **into** (p 79/2 *with preposition*)
116. (which / that) ... **at** (p 79/2 *with preposition*)
117. whose (p 78/1 *2. Fall*)
118. **in / on** which (p 79/2 *with preposition*)
119. (who / that) ... **for** (p 78/1 *with preposition*)
120. **for** whom (p 78/1 *with preposition*)
121. who / that (p 78/1 *1. Fall*)
122. (which / that) (p 79/2 *4. Fall*)
123. (who / that) ... **to** (p 78/1 *with preposition*)
124. (which / that) (p 79/2 *4. Fall*)
125. whose (p 78/1 *2. Fall*)
126. (which / that) ... **to** (p 79/2 *with preposition*)
127. (that), (that) (p 80/3a)
128. whose (p 79/2 *2. Fall*)
129. whose (p 78/1 *2. Fall*)
130. who / that (p 78/1 *1. Fall*)
131. whose (p 78/1 *2. Fall*)
132. (that) (p 80/3a)
133. (which / that) (p 79/2 *4. Fall*)
134. (whom / who / that) (p 78/1 *4. Fall*)
135. (which / that) (p 79/2 *4. Fall*)
136. (who / that) ... **from** (p 78/1 *with preposition*)
137. **from** whom (p 78/1 *with preposition*)
138. (which / that) ... **on** (p 79/2 *with preposition*)
139. (that) (p 80/3a)
140. which (p 81/4)
141. that (p 80/3a)
142. that (p 80/3a)
143. (that) (p 80/3a)
144. what (p 81/5)
145. what (p 81/5), (that) (p 80/3a)
146. what (p 81/5)
147. which (p 81/4)
148. **after** whom (p 78/1 *with preposition*)
149. (who / that) ... **after** (p 78/1 *with preposition*)
150. whose (p 78/1 *2. Fall*)
151. that / who (p 78/1 *1. Fall*)
152. whose (p 79/2 *2. Fall*)

pages 87, 88

1. himself
2. herself
3. himself
4. ourselves (*Kommt, amüsieren wir uns!*)
5. herself
6. herself
7. each other (p 86)
8. himself
9. X (p 87, *Attention*)
10. X (p 87, *Attention*)
11. herself
12. X (p 87, *Attention*)
13. herself
14. X (p 87, *Attention*)
15. himself
16. myself
17. himself (*hier soll betont werden, dass er den Ring für sich selbst kaufte*)
18. X
19. myself (*Ich denke, ich werde mir ein Cola holen.*)
20. himself (*... machte alles in seinem Haus allein.*)
21. himself
22. yourself / yourselves (*Viel Vergnügen!*)
23. himself (*Er sollte besser auf sich aufpassen.*)
24. themselves
25. yourself / yourselves
26. himself
27. himself (*Er weiß nicht, wie er sich benehmen soll.*)
28. herself
29. himself
30. myself
31. X (p 87, *Attention*)
32. each other (p 86)
33. myself
34. himself
35. herself
36. X (p 87, *Attention*)
37. each other (p 86)
38. yourself / yourselves
39. herself
40. myself (*Lass mich selbst sehen.*)
41. himself
42. yourself / yourselves (*Bitte bediene dich / bedienen Sie sich ...*)
43. X (p 87, *Attention*)
44. herself (*Sie möchte jetzt alleine leben ...*)
45. himself
46. itself
47. X (p 87, *Attention*)
48. yourself (*Versuche ganz einfach du zu sein.*)
49. ourselves
50. ourselves
51. themselves
52. X (p 87, *Attention*)
53. ourselves (*... dürfen wir uns noch mit Kuchen bedienen?*)
54. X (p 87, *Attention*)
55. herself (*Sie stellte sich ihren neuen Nachbarn vor.*)
56. himself
57. myself
58. herself

pages 92, 93

Wir verwenden das **by-Objekt** *nur, wenn man den Handelnden* **ganz besonders hervorheben** *will. Achtung auf die Wortstellung!* **Zeitbestimmungen** *stehen* **am Ende oder Anfang** *des Satzes.*

1. Her baby brother was looked *after*. (p 91/F)
2. The thief will be caught.
3. We will be invited by Sharon to her ...
4. This castle was built ... (p 91/E)
5. A letter is going to be written (by me).
6. His house was broken *into*. (p 91/E,F)
7. The fire could be seen far away. (p 90/Modal verbs)
8. We were woken up by the terrible noise.
9. The town was destroyed during the war.
10. Cheese and butter are made from milk.
11. Your ring will be lost if ...
12. Her homework hasn't been done yet.
13. She can be sent a big birthday present. A big birthday present can be sent *to her*. (p 91/D)
14. We may be invited. (p 91/E)
15. The drinks were shaken by the barkeeper.
16. The correct answer hasn't been found yet (by us).
17. The children were allowed by Mr Smith to play ...
18. Lunch won't be cooked by mother today.
19. The house is being painted.
20. My blouse must be ironed.
21. The sandwiches should not be eaten (by the pupils) during the lessons.
22. Bananas and oranges must be imported.
23. The smoke could be seen far away.
24. His room is kept very tidy (by Tom).
25. Some sandwiches have already been made (by him).
26. We were woken up by a terrible noise in the street.
27. The old road was being repaired in the last holidays. (p 91/E)
28. The dustbins are emptied every ... (p 91/E)
29. The old oak tree hasn't been cut down yet.
30. I was angry because the parcel had been sent to the wrong address. (p 91/E)
31. The postman was bitten by our neighbour's dog.
32. Their house in the mountains is going to be sold. (p 91/E)
33. Fred's nose was punched by the bully.
34. The old garden fence is being repaired and painted (by him).
35. The beds must be made before the guests come.
36. I was given a book for my birthday by Simon. A book was given *to me* for my birthday by Simon. (p 91/D)
37. In England school uniforms must be worn.
38. Lunch wasn't prepared by father yesterday.
39. In winter lots of fruit will be eaten (by us) because of ...
40. Smoking isn't allowed in public places. (p 91/E)
41. His car was stolen while ... (p 91/E)
42. I was not sure if I would be offered a better job. I was not sure if a better job would be offered *to me*. (p 91/D, p 91/E)
43. You won't be allowed to use Sue's car. / You won't be allowed by Sue to use her car.
44. On Saturday this shop isn't opened before nine. (p 91/E)

45. Children mustn't be shouted *at*. (p 91/F)
46. Mrs Brown was taken to hospital. (p 91/E)
47. We were shown Oliver's new mountain bike. /
    We were shown his new mountain bike by Oliver.
    Oliver's new mountain bike was shown *to us*.
    (p 91/D)
48. Smoking is not permitted at school.
49. A speech will be given by the headmaster at the beginning ...
50. All the sweets were eaten *up* by little Peter. (p 91/F)
51. The new computer may be used (by you).
52. The water couldn't be turned *off*. (p 91/F)
53. She has been invited to the party.
54. The new words ought to be learnt / learned by heart (by you).
55. The cows and the pigs are being fed by the farmer.
56. The headmaster should have been informed.
57. A pupil is being examined by Mr Stone.
58. The letters will be delivered by a new postman tomorrow.
59. The boxes can be stored over there. (p 90/Modal verbs)
60. The homework mustn't be copied (by you).
61. Those trousers cannot be worn. They ...
62. The children needn't be helped (by you).
63. This job must be applied *for* by Paul. (p 91/F)
64. Oranges are exported. (kein by-object; p 91/E)
65. Do as you are told.
66. The grass was cut (by us) yesterday afternoon.
67. All their problems could be solved. (p 91/E)
68. The cars were parked in the garage. (kein by-object; p 91/E).
69. The cows are being milked by farmer John.
70. They should be given the right to vote. (p 90/Modal verbs)
71. His book was taken out of his satchel. (p 91/E)
72. The rubber boat was hidden somewhere. (p 91/E)
73. The new furniture will be brought tomorrow./ Tomorrow the new ... (p 91/E)
74. A test was being written when the headmaster came in. (p 91/E)
75. Your presents may be opened now.
76. A flat will be bought by our neighbours in Vienna.
77. The window may be shut now.
78. The passive voice can't be used in this case.
79. The disease would have spread if the medicine hadn't been found. (p 91/E)
80. The shoes were made by hand. That's why ... (p 90/B)

SMILE READING COMPREHENSIONS 3

Im modernen Englisch-Unterricht wird auf das Verständnis von Texten großer Wert gelegt, schon ab dem ersten Lernjahr! Konzentration und Aufmerksamkeit sind gefragt, um das Gelesene verstehen und Inhalte verwerten zu können.

- Bedachtnahme auf die **verschiedenen Arten von Leseverständnis**: **schnelles** Lesen (skimming / scanning) einerseits, **detailgenaues** Lesen (careful reading) andererseits.

- **Verschiedenste Textsorten, praxisbezogen und abwechslungsreich:**
  Dialog, Anweisung, Rezept, Einladung, Artikel, Wetterbericht, Geschichte, Fernsehprogramm, E-Mail, Brief, Gedicht, Interview etc.

- Möglichkeit der Selbstkontrolle am Ende des Werkes (**Key**).

Schulbuchnummer 170670
ISBN 978-3-7074-1624-4

SMILE LISTENING COMPREHENSIONS 3

Verstehen, was in einer fremden Sprache gesprochen wird – das ist ein großes Thema im aktuellen Fremdsprachenunterricht!
Schon ab dem 1. Lernjahr muss das Hörverständnis trainiert werden!

Smile Listening Comprehensions bietet zu den einzelnen Hörbeispielen zahlreiche Übungen, die zeigen, ob die Schülerin / der Schüler den gehörten Text verstanden und sich gemerkt hat:

- Einfüllübungen
- True/False-Entscheidungen
- Aus mehreren vorgegebenen Lösungen die passende auswählen und vieles mehr

ISBN 978-3-7074-2184-2

www.ggverlag.at